# REMEMBERING THE SWEET NECTAR

# REMEMBERING THE SWEET NECTAR

*Susanna K. Green*

SWEET NECTAR PUBLISHING

ISBN: 978-0-615-64890-3

SWEET NECTAR PUBLISHING

Copyright Registration Number: TXu-1-600-984

*For my father Rev. Albert Green, my mother Diane (RIP), stepmother Martha and my wonderful sisters, Tita, Rhonda and Jamell; also, my brother Russell and my son Matthew. I love you all.*

# Contents

# Prologue

It was the middle of the week, hump day Wednesday, and there we were once again up to our old antics. Before we jumped on the road, we stopped at the neighborhood liquor store to stock up on beverages to put in our brand-spanking new Styrofoam cooler for our road trip. We headed to the beach for some fun in the sun for the day. This was just one of the many adventures that my two best friends Gina, Kayla and I took several times a year together. It was the spur of the moment, as usual. We hopped in Gina's candy-apple red convertible Eclipse, bumped the music up loud, put the top down and hit the Interstate.

The eighteen-wheelers were on Interstate 10 in large numbers. We were ready and anxious for them to pass us by so that we could gesture to them to honk their horns for us. Every one of them honked because we gave them a first-class reason to.

I decided to get the party started. I positioned my knees in my seat just right, bent over, and mooned a flatbed rolling by. I showed him my shiny silver dental floss thong from the passenger's seat. Kayla followed my lead, taking out her voluptuous double D's, holding them in her hands and sucking her dark brown, quarter sized areolas in the back seat. Gina struggled to drive steadily in our lane while laughing hysterically at the truckers' reactions. One trucker honked his horn excessively and then got on his CB radio to alert his fellow truckers. The next thing we knew the road was flooded with drivers trying to get an eye-full. Unfortunately, we had to walk by at least fifteen trucks on our way into the truck stop just to get to the entrance to use the rest room. We had not been on the road for a good thirty minutes when already our drinks had run right through us. We had hoped that we wouldn't see any of the drivers that we had tantalized along the way, so we hurried. We did not want propositions or to be mistaken for lot-lizards just because we were having a little harmless fun.

Kayla, Gina, and I playfully fought over this one stall in particular. It was the cleanest one. They ran in before me so I gave it up and let them have first dibs. As I walked further toward the back stalls, I saw an elderly woman wearing pink sponge rollers in her hair, on the toilet in a stall without a door. She sat with her elbows drooping on her wide-open knees and her sweat pants hanging around her ankles, defecating. She seemed to be enjoying it because she made some nasty stomach-churning sounds of relief. I changed my mind about using the restroom; instead, I turned around, squeezed my nostrils together, and headed for the door because of my weak stomach. I waited for the girls' right outside of the lavatory until they came out.

After they freshened up a bit, we hopped back in the car and continued toward our destination. It was only a short ride to where we were going, but by the time we reached Biloxi, Mississippi, I knew most of the words to the new India Irie and Maxwell CD's because Gina kept alternating them repeatedly. We made a U-turn and got back on the highway. Shortly after, Gina spotted a cute guy who resembled Morris Chestnut whom she referred to as her next victim in the rear view mirror that she decided she wanted to tease. She had a smirk on her face. She slowed down to allow him to catch up so she could make eye contact with him. Her plan fell right into place just as fast as the idea popped into her head.

Sure enough, the young stud slowly cruised up next to us. Gina smiled and batted her false eyelashes at him. He rolled his passenger side window down, lowered his rap music so they could chat a little bit over the crisp wind. He asked for her phone number, but she wanted to talk to him in person so she spontaneously told him to follow us off the next exit. Gina kept peeping through her Versace knock-off sunglasses that she bought on the street from a kiosk stand in order to keep track of him through the rear view mirror. Kayla and I looked back to make sure that he was still following us and he was.

"I love a guy who follows instructions well." Gina said, talking to herself but loud enough for Kayla and me to hear.

We got off at the exit and pulled into a gas station so they could properly make each other's acquaintances. The girls and I waited anxiously for him to walk over to our car so we could get a good laugh. We all started fixing our windblown hair that had been tousling through the breeze to look presentable. I had wondered why we parked in an inconspicuous area, around the backside of the gas station. As soon as the nameless male walked up to us, Gina seductively asked him if he liked what he saw. Before he could answer, she grabbed him by his collar with one hand, aggressively pulled him up against the side of the car, and started kissing him in the mouth. Kayla was the freakiest of the bunch. She pulled down her spandex tank top and whipped out her best assets, her breasts. She let them loosely hang down on the outside of the car. She kneeled on her seat and leaned over the car door, unzipped his pants, dug her way through the hole in his boxer shorts, and started kissing his swelling manhood. It quickly inflated and stood at attention like a Marine at a fellow soldier's funeral. I felt left out so I figured that I should find a way to participate. I leaned over Gina, pulled up his Polo shirt with the green alligator on the left side and commenced to sucking his already hard and hairy left nipple. His knees appeared weak as he stood there letting us have our way with him. He didn't utter a single word, just sighs, and moans of delight. His eyes were wide open like a deer caught in the headlights, as if he didn't want to miss a single second of what was happening to him. We pleasured him for approximately two minutes flat when he exploded all over himself and the driver's side door. Gina had her foot on the accelerator and the car started rolling slowly. I fell back in my seat and Kayla did too. Gina yelled, "Bye," waved and screeched off fast. We could hear his voice echoing, "Wait, Wait," standing there with an open fly and a still rock hard penis waving his arms in the air, as if he were signaling for help.

We laughed until tears fell while recapping the episode, still trying to make it to the strip of the sandy beach.

The sirens sounded louder and more defined at the stop sign as the red and blue flashing lights gradually made its way to the back of our car. We heard through a bullhorn "pull your vehicle into the parking lot now!" We all turned our heads and looked behind us to discover a hillbilly police officer staring at us as if we were common criminals. The laughter ceased and uneasy feelings took over.

"I'm not pulling over."

"What? You have to pull over, especially after he told you to. We could get in big trouble, girl," I said.

"I'm telling you, I ain't pulling over. Something don't feel right."

"I don't know Gee. I'm with Reina on this one. He's not gonna give up and leave. We'll eventually have to pull over anyway. Just pull over and see what he wants," Kayla insisted.

"Yeah, we can't just keep driving like we don't hear him yelling at us through that damn bullhorn Gina. Just please pull over."

Gina pulled into the vacant parking lot by an uninhabited building as he instructed her. There was dead silence amongst us as we waited for the officer to make his way to Gina's side of the car. We wondered what he could possibly want. Gina wasn't speeding and she didn't run any red lights or stop signs.

He approached Gina's side and asked to see her license, registration, and proof of insurance. He seemed pleasantly surprised that we were not from around the Mississippi parts. He told Gina to step out of the car and go back to his squad car with him so that he could get some information from her. He told her to get in the front seat while he ran her name. Kayla and I waited patiently until she came back but she never did.

I wondered what was taking so long. The shifty eyed officer finally walked back to our car and instructed us all to go back to his car with him so that he could run our names as well. He made us all sit in the front seat with him because he said that the back doors were not operable at the time, which I thought was extremely bizarre. We cooperated because he was a police officer. Gina apprehensively scooted over towards him and we crammed in behind her. He locked the doors, drove forward about ten feet, and parked the passenger side of the car right up against the back wall of the building. He turned off his dispatch radio and then pointed his glock at our heads and told us to do to him exactly what we had done to the guy at the gas station ten miles back.

We didn't realize we were being followed. We didn't even see him anywhere around the vicinity but apparently, he saw us. There was no denying it if he was telling us what he saw. He said that he would let us slide with a warning this time but we would have to repay him in favors.

Gina had a look of terror on her face and Kayla started rambling. She acted as if she didn't know what he was talking about. I sat frantically waiting to see what the girls would do first. I kept discreetly looking around for a way out of the car but it was jammed up so closely against the building that the door would not be able to open. He held the gun in his left hand and unzipped his pants with his right. He forced Gina's hand on his private spot and told her to suck it, she refused so he yelled louder, "SUCK IT, or I'll kill all you bitches right now."

Gina went down on him with tears welling in her eyes. She nervously licked around his pale tinctured shaft area but he was not satisfied with that. He violently shoved her head down lower until she unwillingly received a mouth full and sucked it to his satisfaction. When he was almost to a climatic state, he grabbed Gina by the hair, raised her off him, and told Kayla that it was her turn so she just went at it. He said, "That's right, that's how you did it to him wasn't it?" "I watched you and you liked it, didn't you?" "Suck me harder, like you sucked him"! Her strategy was to be agreeable, instead of struggling with him. The sooner she got it over with the sooner we could get out of there. Still pointing the gun at us, he forcefully rammed Kayla's head down as hard as he could and climaxed deep in the back of her throat. She made the sound of the gag reflex and then he let her up.

The unwanted juices dripped from her bottom lip as she continued to gag in an effort to catch her breath. He paused and then looked at me to go next. I silently prayed that he didn't force himself on me like he had done my girlfriends but from the look in his eyes, even though he had climaxed already and had gone limp, he wanted me to suffer too, just because.

"Mmm, I saved the best for last," he said, grabbing my hair, shoving me down to where his little wilted meat sat and smashed my face right into it. When I smelled all of the saliva mixed with his sweaty scrotum scent it made me sick to my stomach. I couldn't control the curdled regurgitation that came from deep within me. As soon as I let out the smelly contents of my sour stomach all over his lightly starched uniform pants, he forcefully pushed me away and said, "Aw, look whatchu don done now you little bitch, look whatchu don done."

Terror set in!

"If any of you bitches say anything about this to anybody, I'm comin to all your houses one by one and kill you and your family too. You hear me?"

We shook our heads in agreement because we knew he had our personal information.

He quickly drove forward and unlocked the doors to throw us out of his car.

"Get the hell outta my car," he adamantly shouted.

We quickly hopped back in the convertible and drove off. We could not believe what had just happened. I was mortified! I had prayed the whole time that God would spare our lives and I vowed never to do anything like we had done to a strange man ever again. God mercifully answered my prayers and spared our lives just as I had desperately asked him to do. I was relieved that we were all still alive, at least.

Gina was the most shook up; she even talked about putting a hit out on him. I told her that I could tell my Uncle Seth and he and his boys would kill him. Kayla was just glad it was finished. I thought that we should still tell the authorities but then I didn't want to put our lives at risk, either. My emotions were running so high. I wasn't thinking clearly. My heart raced as I sat in my seat gazing out of the window. Gina cut a corner to the right so fast without using her blinker; we hit a curb and then tilted in that direction. She rushed us in to a Pizza Hut where we went into the bathroom to wash our mouths out and clean ourselves up. I felt disgusted by the whole thing. There was no way that we could go and sit on the beach and have a good time after what had just occurred, so we just decided to head back home. Honestly, I didn't have an appetite at all, but I knew that I should have probably put something on my completely empty stomach from the sound of the growl it made.

We spotted a few hotels along the strip that would have been perfect for our lodging needs but we all agreed that our fun was down the drain at that point.

Gina put the top up on the convertible. I gazed out of the tinted windows thinking on the day's events and wondering how that crooked cop could sleep peacefully at night. I thought everybody had a conscience. Even though I hated what had happened to my girls back there I couldn't help but think how happy I was that it didn't happen to me.

It was a short drive home because Gina sped most of the way back. We made a pact that we would not speak a word of what happened to anybody, ever. We even shook on it. Ten years later it remained the same, what happened on that beautifully sunny day in the muddy Mississippi stayed in Mississippi. God always seemed to favor me, particularly when I got myself into bad situations and that was yet another one of those times that I knew he was not pleased. I silently thanked him for praying parents.

# Chapter 1

It was feverishly hot outside as I strolled through City Park soaking up the picture perfect presence of God's creation for my daily exercise routine; entailing a little preparatory stretching, then slow walking which evolved into a jog. I usually spent about an hour or two a day tending to my physical person. I surprisingly found it to be great mental exercise as well. It cleansed my mind and freed my spirit from the daily noise of life, a nirvana, indeed! It allowed for some desperately needed "me" time.

I could permit my mind to just be idle and not have to share myself with anyone, or consider anybody else's needs. Yep, it was all about me when I was out there running and panting. I loved the smell of the fresh hibiscus flowers in bloom, especially during spring, and the nice cool gentle wind I felt from sitting by the pond under the trees. However, that particular day in the heart of summer, very hot, humid and muggy, I felt a brush of air, almost like a breeze, if I walked at a speedy pace under the trees. I sensed my body dehydrating, so I stopped at the nearest water fountain to replenish. The water was so hot that I should have brought my herbal green-tea bags.

I found a pond where a few ducks were, sat and listened to them incessantly make that God-awful quacking sound, while kicking my bare feet back and forth in the water. I took my leather fanny pack from around my waist, put it under my sweaty head, and lay back onto the neatly manicured grass to catch my breath and wait for my body temperature to regress. Out of my
peripheral vision, I caught a glance of an obviously in-love couple who wore blue and white Nike matching shorts sets, jogging side by

side while the husband ran with their light brown cocker spaniel on an extendable leash. The wife pushed their twins in a doublewide stroller. I watched them until they were out of sight when I felt myself drifting away with my thoughts.

I was exhausted, but decided not to leave the park yet. I still had six more pounds to lose. I promised myself that I would dedicate two measly hours a day toward my goal.

My Louisiana-native husband Lance bought me a brand-new dress to wear to our annual Fourth of July dance. What a beautiful silk and lace, black, spaghetti strapped mini it was. That dress captured the essence of every curve I didn't know I had. Lance was faultless when it came to picking out clothes and jewelry for me. I had no desire to return any of his gifts. He had impeccable taste. He also knew that a woman's weight could sometimes fluctuate, so to be sure he went with the sizes that I currently wore when he bought clothes for me. He was thoughtful in that regard. Since he had gone through the trouble of making sure that I had the perfect dress, the least I could do was make sure I was flawless while wearing it. Therefore, two hours of an adrenaline rush a day was, in my mind, me doing my part to continue looking good for my man.

Lance was always big on presentation. I came home one day to find my fabulous gift in the center of our enormous king-sized bed that he bought us for our first year anniversary. It was enhanced with big blood-red rose petals and a note written on a piece of beautifully flowered stationary paper that read, "Just because". I was so excited I beamed. I could have actually screamed to the top of my lungs. I would have, if it weren't for fear that our meddlesome neighbors in the condominiums next door would dial 911. Therefore, I kept my composure and swaggered over to the mirror. I held the thin, dainty piece of material up to my soft, creamy caramel-colored skin and smiled at the thought of how radiant I would look at the party while hobnobbing. I've always prided myself on being the very best at everything I did. That included outdoing all of the other women there.

I had a beauty regimen that I followed whenever I wanted to be an absolute stunning glamour-pus. That involved Enrique trimming and styling my hair. Then, Liz would give me a micro-derm abrasion facial, to remove all of my dead skin cells. Jarvis soothed me with a full body massage. One of the Asian girls in the back would polish my nails and finally, Judy waxed my . . . well that stayed between Judy and me.

The dress certainly came at the perfect time. Lance knew exactly what he was doing. Every time he stayed out too late or didn't follow through with what he said, he tried to make up for it by buying me gifts. I must admit I liked the little surprises and gifts at first, but it got old very quickly. I even came to expect it. He had become too predictable. I knew his moves before he made them. He constantly had to be doing something. From day one, I should have noticed my first clue. He spread himself as thin as butter that had been sitting out all night.

We met up at my favorite local uptown coffee house. We weren't there ten minutes when his phone started ringing off the hook. He didn't answer the first few calls, but the callers became persistent. The first call he received was from his drunken Uncle Duke who asked Lance to come to the lower ninth ward and help him change his alternator in that old raggedy pick-up truck that usually sat broken down in his driveway.

The second call was from his hysterical Aunt Mae who needed Lance to play the role of referee. Her two roughneck sons were fighting in her apartment in the Magnolia Housing Project and tore up all of her furniture, again.

Then there was Mama Pearl. His mama called to have Lance pick up a "few" things from the grocery store. He asked me if I would go with him, so I did. We arrived at the grocery store approximately fifteen minutes from the time they last spoke. We must have picked up about forty items while being instructed every step of the way by Mama Pearl on the other end of the phone. She wanted to ensure that he got the exact named brand items that she usually bought. Initially,

I found it sweet how Lance catered to his mother but little did I know how much he was in fact wrapped around her little old-lady finger.

Lance was a good person, and people knew that, so they took advantage of him. I sometimes told him when I thought someone was using him. He said he didn't care about any of that because that was how he got his blessings, by helping people. I knew he was right, still it made me mad that people regularly called on my man, all of the time. Maybe I was just being selfish. At least that was what I told myself for three years, until I realized I wasn't.

Lance was all over the place, solving this one or that one's problem. He started having less and less time for me. I was his wife, for God's sake. I suddenly realized why people cheated on one another. It didn't feel good and I refused to sit around feeling sorry for myself. Although Lance had a wonderful spirit and an amazing sense of humor, a lot of good it did; he wasn't home long enough for me to experience any of it. I was tired of being alone. I wanted my man in the house and accounted for. Instead, he was probably in the ninth ward across the canal at his mother's house. If I didn't know any better, I would have thought that I was jealous of his mother, but I knew better. Ms. Pearl never liked me anyway, as far as I was concerned. Lance said she did, but I knew his ulterior motive was to keep the peace and diffuse the situation at any cost, including telling me a bold faced lie. Every time he and I got into an argument, he ran over to her house. I didn't think it was healthy. No wonder she was always in our business. I asked him to keep our problems just between us, but he and Pearl were very close, especially since he found out she was diabetic and then his father died.

I turned onto my left side, getting more comfortable as I continued thinking about Lance, our relationship and life in general.

His father was a man of the world, a ladies-man of sorts. He loved traveling to different countries with the military and experiencing their cultures, even though he was supposed to be there on business. You know the song, "Papa was a rolling stone, wherever he laid his hat was his home?" Well, that was an understatement. Pearl had a good idea of what was going on, but Lance said she was always so strong and never let him see her in distress. Lance was their only child. It was one big vicious cycle with the two of them. When Pearl became suspicious of what was going on out there overseas, she stopped sleeping with Carl. Not only did she stop being intimate with him, she moved into the guest room. She said she didn't want to catch the VD, as she referred to it. Lance told me that his mother said the reason Carl stepped outside of their marriage was that she didn't want to satisfy his manly needs. Through it all, she never talked bad about her husband to her son. She quietly lugged around her pain in order to make sure Lance knew the saga of his father's heroics. Carl had earned all kinds of medals of Honor during his time in the military. He was an admirable soldier.

While doing the latter part of his twelve-year stint in the army he contracted hepatitis from one of the women in Korea. He swore he did not know which woman in particular gave it to him, because there had been so many. He said for the most part he used condoms. He admitted there were a few occasions where they either slipped off or popped. He remorsefully confessed to Pearl when he and a couple more of his fellow soldiers were discharged from the service for getting caught receiving oral pleasures from a couple of the women in a brothel. He displayed unbecoming conduct of a soldier. Therefore, he was relieved of his duties.

Carl wanted to set the record straight and get right with the Lord when he found out his health status, so he finally told her everything he had done behind her back. He told her that he had been with so many women he could no longer keep track of them all. He said they were mostly of Asian descent though, as if that was supposed to be some sort of consolation. Carl told her that these women would do absolutely anything you wanted them to do for only a few dollars. He said that it did not take away from the love he had for her, but he was out there in the middle of nowhere and didn't want to appear to be a chump to his peers. He even went as far as to tell her that since it went against her religious beliefs to participate in the oral part of their sex life that he had begged for, for years, he had to get it else-where because he loved it so much. He said all the young girls were doing it and he didn't understand why she wouldn't at least try it.

Carl admitted to his wife things that the average person would have taken with them to their grave but he felt the need to come completely clean with her. He wanted to get it all off his chest. No more secrets. He said many of the soldiers participated in those kinds of activities; they just never got caught by testing positive on one of the blood tests that the military randomly administered. Unfortu-nately, there was no cure for what he had contracted.

Carl and Pearl had their problems but she stuck in there with him until his dying day. Pearl evidently took her vows very seriously. She took her husband home after the doctors at the VA hospital said there was nothing else they could do for him. She spoon-fed him as she did Lance when he was a baby. She changed his diapers when he was no longer able to make it to the bathroom. She read the Bible to him every morning and every night; held his hand until he fell asleep. She prayed with and for him when he could no longer pray for himself. That's how our parents and especially our grandparent's generation dealt with things. They stuck it out through thick and thin, no matter what. I admired Ms. Pearl for being able to muster up the strength to care for a man unconditionally who took their love for granted. He put her life at risk and she still concerned herself with him. My generation is so far off from the true meaning of marriage that we would divorce our spouses for snoring too loudly or leaving the toilet seat up, like many couples I know.

In a way, I envied his relationships with his family because I was mentally detached from mine. At birth, a Christian couple took me in. My foster parents could not have any children. Father was sterile. We had many problems in our home that hindered us from being a close-knit family. My adopted father, Reverend William J. Singleton was the proud pastor of a quaint little church in Memphis. He wore a distinguished-looking salt and pepper beard naturally matching the hairs on his head. He and my refined adopted mother, Lorraine M.

Singleton, took up residency there after moving from Woodville Mississippi. Her only job was to be the first lady of the church and his lovely wife. She was always dressed to impress and wore very fine hats to the services. She sat on the front pew waving a white handkerchief in the air, clapping and agreeably nodding at everything father said, shouting "Preach Pastor" every chance she got. She and Pops stuck together like white on rice. I just couldn't seem to live up to all of their rigid expectations. The fact that I came home one day with a small tattoo of a butterfly on my right ankle was the last straw for them. I could not stand it anymore. They constantly told me how secular and sinful I was, so I left home at seventeen and started a life of my own.

I turned toward the life I had always dreamed of. I dated just about every type of man on the continuum. After playing the trophy role to a few NFL players, a Musician and a CEO, I met Lance. Financially, he took good care of me; I didn't have to lift a finger or open my purse for a dime. I guess that's why I stayed with him for so long. I had nowhere else to go. My family did not have anything to offer me in life, except their inflexible version of love; unfortunately, that just was not enough. However, over time, I came to realize that money wasn't everything. I was restless and lacked peace of mind. Lance was all I had but he was all over the place. I just wish he didn't have to save the whole world. I was lonely. When he was gone, I missed him, but when we were together, he worked my nerves harder than a roustabout working on an oilrig. He had me right where he wanted me, or so he thought, until I figured out his motive, which was to control me. He didn't know what I was up to at any given moment. I liked it like that. I had him baffled. Our relationship had become one big game. The only thing I could do was play to win. Lance had my mind gone for a long time but I must say, I have proven to be more resourceful than either of us would have thought.

I loved Lance with all my heart but I had to accept things as they were, bleak. I settled for that way of life for a long time because of that love but I knew I wanted so much more. His absence, in retrospect, gave me a second chance to get to know myself all over again. So much so, I started taking self-help classes at a leisure center in the central business district, once a week. After only three classes, I realized that Lance was holding me back from the true happiness I yearned for; happiness I knew I deserved. I needed somebody to hold me and let me be free to be me. Lance made me feel like a queen as long as everything went his way. It was his way or the highway because he paid all of the bills. Nevertheless, when I gave in to him, he treated me like royalty, as long he didn't feel disrespected. That was what he called it when I had any type of conversations with other men. Old, fat, crippled or dying, he swore they wanted me. He alleged I must have liked the attention, because I entertained it which was the most ridiculous thing I had ever heard. Nonetheless, to Lance, it was an extremely big deal. In the beginning, the jealousy was somewhat cute. It let me know he cared about me. Yet, little did I know it would get worse over time and on certain occasions, in particular, it was not endearing at all.

Raised as a military brat, Lance learned to like things orderly. When things were not organized he became intolerant and acted out of character. When we argued, he left the house. I needed a way out. Even though our relationship took a turn for the worse, I still managed to have a sense of self worth and confidence that exuded all throughout me. I actually liked going to those meetings. I met some positive people there who seemed to have a genuine interest in me.

My job sucked, though. I did not have a heartfelt passion for re-upholstering furniture. I was quite good at it and people bought it, just, no passion. It was all Lance's idea that I take a position there since I quit my previous job in social work to travel the United States with my last boyfriend. I knew I would eventually grow bored with stapling fabric to wood, and I did. I didn't know what I wanted to do with my life. My focus was on Lance's needs. I always did what he wanted and lost sight of my own dreams. Whatever Lance wanted he got, at least from me, which is how I ended up working at the furniture store so he could keep a close eye on me. I was head over heels for that man, and he knew it. He was number one in my life. I had been committed and loyal. He was as happy and content as a pig in slop. It just wasn't enough for me anymore. Maybe I was just too high maintenance for him. I required more than a silky black dress, the bills paid, and a good lay once a week. I needed much more.

On that particular day as I lay relaxing on the ground, I decided to indulge myself in a clandestine affair of the heart, with no one in particular in mind. Just covertly knowing I entertained the idea was a thousand pounds lifted off my shoulders. I thought about going down to the spa and have Jarvis give me one of his fantastic hot stone shiatsu rubdowns while I paid full attention to all of the understated details to get the maximum enjoyment. Watching the way his pearly whites glistened and illuminated the room when he softly spoke to me during our consultation about any problems I might be having in my body. The way he salaciously flirted with his eyes, but remaining very professional when he instructed me to disrobe and cover with the soft downy cotton sheet. The way his big chocolate hands would feel as he rubbed that hot lavender hemp seed oil up, down, and all over my body. The sensation of his peppermint-flavored breath grazing the small of my back as he gently leaned over me to apply more pressure. Last, but not least, the connection I felt with him when he transferred his energy into me by way of a reiki treatment.

I had to fan myself after escalating my own heart rate by fantasizing about all the erotic things that Jarvis would do to me once he got me into that little faintly lit room of his. It had come time to stop dreaming and execute that plan. I felt like being adventurous, even if it was . . . only in my mind. What Lance didn't know wouldn't hurt him. What Jarvis didn't know . . . well, I intended to keep my fantasies under wraps, for the time being anyway. It amazed me that I had never even noticed him in a magnetic way before, during one of my prior sessions. He's such a handsome man, almost my age, twenty-nine, and six feet tall. He had a thin athletic build, and toned in all the right places. It was something about the way his biceps screamed for air through his bluish-green Abercrombie pullover. It hugged him so tightly and perfectly matched his eyes. He always left me wanting more. Jarvis had the most alluring eyes I had ever seen even though I pretended not to look into them during our sessions. I wondered why my pulse had never raced, my knees ever buckled, or my womanhood ever throbbed for him. Lance, he had my heart, my full-undivided attention, my commitment, my loyalty and respect. I think I even gave up my soul. Some people sold their soul to the devil, but not me. I just gave mine away free; to a man, who thought all he had to do was buy me nice gifts to keep me satisfied. I must say. I fell for it, at first. I fell hard, until I realized what he was doing. You see, if all had gone right and Lance's heartfelt gifts were sincere and genuine, I would have felt as if I had gotten something out of the deal. However, because they always came with a price, I felt in actuality, I really accomplished nothing. In return, what did Lance get? He got a bitter wife who resented him to the core. That same resentment has allowed for the door now to be open to explore the silent, yet eloquent world of love...real Love, true love.

"Miss," said the pudgy, freckle faced, snagged tooth boy, feeding the ducks.

I heard his little voice and opened my eyes, from my daydream.

"Miss, are you okay?" he asked, concerned.

"Yeah, I'm okay. Thank you for checking on me, my baby," I smiled.

The young boy grinned back at me and continued feeding torn slices of bread to the ducks. I was in a deep trance when he came over to me. I collected myself and rolled onto my knees for support. I pushed myself up and stood there gazing into space until I felt comfortable resuming my exercise. All of the perspiration on my body had evaporated and I was completely relaxed sitting there by the pond, enjoying my thoughts. However, I had six more pounds to lose in less than two weeks. I had to get cracking.

# Chapter 2

"Happy Fourth of July babe," Lance was in good spirits as he blew his breath through the long tube to hear that annoying squeaky noise.

"Right back at you," I grabbed his hand, smiling my Dorothy Dandridge smile.

I looked stunning in my new dress. Everyone complemented me as I ever-so gracefully sashayed through the clean-cut crowd to mingle. I knew losing those six pounds would set me over the top. Lance and I slow danced to a couple of mellow songs. I loved the annual Fourth of July bashes. It always seemed to bring us closer. Lance held me snug to him as his hands rested gently on my lower waistline. He enjoyed taking the lead when we danced. He was so good at it and I enjoyed it as much as he did. Dancing was definitely one of Lance's most promising qualities. I didn't know what I liked most, his sensual moves, the way he enveloped me so tenderly within his embrace or the way my body naturally extracted warmth from his; whatever caused me to melt like a candle burning at both ends in his arms every time he held me close, I loved it. It quite possibly could have been just an old-fashioned case of being in love, although I felt like I was on a roller coaster ride at Six Flags. Who knew how I would feel later. It was as if my love was in a constant state of flux, and that was not good. If someone didn't know me well, they could mistake me for being schizophrenic, or even bipolar. Still, I am neither. I just have a very keen sense of what I want in a man.

At the party Lance was a perfect gentleman. He had the greatest gift for making me feel like the only woman in the room. I feel like a princess when I'm with him. That's why I married him.

"Babe,"

"Yes love,"

"Seriously, where have you been all my life?" Lance asked, while looking directly into my water-filled eyes.

"Waiting for you,"

"I hope those are happy tears," he said, dabbing his index knuckle in the corner of my left eye, which he must have thought would be the first tear to fall.

"They are babe; they are."

"Well in that case, carry on then," he said, playfully.

I couldn't help feeling mesmerized. Lance quickened the beat of my heart with every word he spoke. All of my prior thoughts about what Jarvis could do to me vanished. All I wanted at that moment was some miraculous power to improve my relationship. Therefore, we continued our slow-dance and I quietly said a little prayer to purge me from all of the malevolent thoughts that I had allowed to enter my mind. Deep down I knew Lance was my only passion.

I liked the fact that Lance didn't care what other people thought of him. He did his own thing and I found that trait so sexy, except when he did it for the wrong reasons. He didn't care that a few of his fraternity brothers were at the party, possibly watching him act insanely crazy about me. He didn't do the typical thing that guys do when they know they're being watched by the fellas, try to look cool. He just carried on with me as if they weren't even there. I liked that he didn't try to impress all of those losers by pretending to be uncon-cerned about me. What woman wouldn't? Men generally don't like to classify themselves as being in love . . . having their noses open . . . or carrying a torch, but not Lance. It was almost as if he got off on being different. Lance did not mind exhibiting public displays of affection. In fact, we would walk through the mall, looking at clothes or some-thing and "bamm", right upside my unsuspecting lips; He would plant a passionate kiss on me right there, in the middle of the store. I used to get embarrassed until I decided it was no use. He had done it so much it all started to seem normal. I could never figure out though, what the animated dramatizations were all about. One day, it all hit me. Like a bag of bricks, I finally saw Lance for who he really was, insecure and controlling.

Looking back, it was all so very clear. Every time Lance showed me a spontaneous display of affection there was undoubtedly another guy somewhere on the scene. It never dawned on me that he was using me to prove a point to other men. It was a macho thing between them. At that moment, I asked myself why men felt they had to prove to each other whose penis was bigger, whose game was tighter, whose manhood was stronger, who had the finest girlfriend; I could go on and on.

When I first had the epiphany, I was in shock. Then, the shock quickly wore off because I realized that I was not as shocked as I thought I was, if that makes any sense. Considering my last few relationships, Lance's issues did not seem so bad, but they were. Those were issues most definitely worth keeping an eye on. Better yet, both eyes. I couldn't see myself leaving, though. That's what happens when you let someone else dictate your life and put you in a position where you can't financially take care of yourself because you're too busy relying on them, you're stuck. Therefore, I did what I always did when I wanted to go, stay. I just crossed my fingers and hoped the night would go as planned.

As we walked away from the dance floor hand in hand, I saw Lance's friend Johnny with a freshly cut fade walking bow-legged toward us.

"Lance Joseph, what's been up whodie?" Johnny said, smiling and reaching out his fist for some dap.

"Johnny, my boy, not a whole lot, I haven't seen you in a few years?" Lance smiled, balling his fist up to meet Johnny halfway.

"I know cuz, I was in Iraq. This is my first time coming to this shindig."

"Awe man, it's always a blast. Good clean fun out here man." You remember my wife Reina huh?"

"How could I forget Miss Reina? You stole her right from under my nose."

"Boy quit playing. You know you never had a chance with all of this," Lance said, doing his Kee Kee Shepherd impersonation, displaying me as the exhibit, still smiling.

"If you say so big L..." Johnny wisecracked, looking at my frame up and down, licking his lips like L.L. Cool J, with a Cheshire grin on his face.

I could not believe what I had heard. Johnny implied to Lance that he had a chance with me. When was this? How dare he stand there and flatter himself like that, at my expense? I started feeling a little unnerved. I wasn't sure if Lance would blow it off or go into anaphylactic shock and then come out swinging because I know hearing Johnny spew those words stung him like a bee. Knowing Lance . . . I should've probably been worried. He didn't let stuff like that go. Oh well. The party was good while it lasted. However, honestly, I had been waiting for the bomb to drop all night. It always did.

"What's that supposed to mean, Johnny?"

"Awe man, don't worry bout it. You got her nah. Don't trip!"

"You can't say something like that and then say, forget about it. That's not cool bruh."

"Whatever man, you don got soft over the years, dawg."

"Soft? You just told me in so many words that my wife wanted to get with you."

"And your point,"

"My point is, you trippin," Lance said stepping in closer, getting in his face, with clenched fists.

"Man, what does it matter anyway, that was three years ago, right?

"Lance, let's go. I can't take any more of Johnny's ego." I grabbed him by the arm. "It's making me sick,"

"Okay, as soon as you tell this fool you didn't want him!"

"Is this really necessary Lance?" I asked, anxiously.

"Yeah, now tell him!" Lance said, as his eyes narrowed and jaws tightened.

"Why are we even entertaining him? He's obviously delusional."

"Is there some reason you don't want to tell him Reina?"

"Johnny knows that he's being ridiculous," I said.

"Yeah Lance, I'm just being ridiculous, just drop it will ya?" Johnny interjected.

"Reina, tell him once and for all that you never wanted him and I'll drop it," He urged, with tense facial muscles and a look of rage.

"Okay, fine. Johnny, I never wanted you!"

"And if she did, why would she say it in front of you? That doesn't make any sense, now does it?" Johnny antagonized.

"Reina's a big girl; she don't have to lie to me."

"Can we leave now, Lance?" I snapped, at the end of my rope.

"Certainly Babe," Lance slowly pulled my face to his and passionately kissed my lips, while giving Johnny a grimacing look. I stood there astonished. I wondered what Lance's next move would be. I stood as still as a picture in a frame, mounted on a wall . . . waiting.

I submissively followed Lance's lead as he guided me toward the bar area, as if nothing had transpired at all. It was almost as if Johnny didn't exist. I almost felt like the ordeal was over, but who was I kidding? Lance didn't work that way.

Surprisingly, after about fifteen minutes of normalcy, my heart rate began to beat at its regular pace and all seemed well.

The crowd slow danced to the smooth sounds of Kem as the bald entertainer stood up center stage and dazzled his audience. The stage had dimmed lighting that engulfed the large number of people gathered together for the elegant event. Lance walked up to the open bar to order our usual, which was a Heineken for him and a Bloody Mary for me. I've always loved a good Bloody Mary, especially with the long, spicy beans.

I went over to the stage to make a request. I wanted to hear "When Love Calls."

City Park looked top notch. I walked around by myself admiring the beautiful scenery when Lance marched up with the drinks.

"What was that about?" Lance asked, handing me my drink.

"What was what?"

"I saw you standing by the stage all in Kem's face and whispering in his ear."

"Oh, yeah baby, I went to make a request. I want to hear 'When Love Calls.' You know that's our jam," I said, sliding in toward him.

"Was that all you'll talked about?" He asked, pushing me away with his free hand.

"Pretty much,"

"What does that mean?"

"It means that I requested a song. " *When Love Calls*," What's the problem Lance?"

"Look, when you are with me, respect me enough not to flirt with other guys, okay?"

"I was not flirting with him, I just req . . ."

Lance walked away, infuriated with me. I was left standing there all alone, holding my bloody Mary with one lousy little bean. "What just happened?" I asked myself. "Hell if I know." Self responded. I felt like all eyes were on me. After that fabulous grand entrance I made, the last thing I wanted was for Lance to reprimand me in front of the bevy of playa-hating females. I was too much of a diva for that so I quickly put on a superficial smile and sucked it up.

While trying to slip away for cover, I spotted Lance over at the bar talking to a scantily clad female who frightfully lacked style, based on that atrocious multi colored twenty seven-piece wig she wore and her gaudy taste in costume jewelry. She was dressed in a short black micro-mini skirt with fish net stockings and stripper pumps with glass heels. She looked like she belonged on the corner of South Central in Los Angeles. Lance was so obvious. He went over to talk to her out of sheer vindictiveness. "I'll play along", I thought to myself. He just kept digging his hole deeper and deeper and he didn't even know it. He went and found the raunchiest girl at the party, trying to make me jealous. She wasn't even his type. He doesn't like girls who look like hookers. He thinks they're nasty. I was not going to allow my nerves to be upset because he was being petty. He called himself trying to give me a taste of my own medicine, when all he did was further push me into wanting to get rid of him for good this time. I banked on having some great material to throw in his face if he kept it up. I wouldn't even have to set him up or pick fake arguments with him. He was doing great all by himself. I was almost as free as a kiss in the wind.

"Keep up the good work, Lance. Yeah, keep talking to that hoochie girl, the longer the better," I thought to myself.

Lance slyly kept looking my way, hoping to catch eyes with me. I intentionally didn't pacify his ego trip but it only made him try harder. Trying to give Lance the constant adoration that he needed had become an excruciating experience for me. It was very sad.

I had a feeling on the ride over that something would go wrong at the party. I couldn't put my finger on it, but I sensed it. I guess I was just over the whole thing, Lance, the relationship, the whole thing.

Maybe, just maybe, I allowed for the scene of me talking to Kem to look like I was flirting, subconsciously, to sabotage our relationship. Maybe my body language spoke the unspoken words of what my imagination was supposed to keep a secret. Maybe Lance knew me, just that well, where he could detect from across a crowded park what my hidden thoughts were. In that case, my thoughts were hidden so well, I didn't even know they were there. I did not flirt with Kem! Lance, in my opinion was so insecure sometimes he created scenarios that were not real. He always accused me of flirting with guys, especially when I wasn't. On the other hand, the times that I have noticed a guy that I found attractive, he never caught it, hmmm!

Lance walked back over to me disappointed that his tactics had not fazed me one bit. I was so proud of myself. I was beating him at his own game and he hated every second of it. Lance was so used to me always bowing down to him that he couldn't handle it when I stood up for myself. I was exemplary. I deserved an Emmy. Maybe I should have looked into some acting classes. I may have missed my calling, fooling around with Lance and that stupid furniture.

I did not mention a single word about Lance's conversation with the female. Lance was quiet, too. I think he was trying to figure out my angle. Still, it was as I always say, "you can't play a playa." That was exactly what he was trying to do, except he kept getting his feelings hurt. Poor Lance.

"This was for the lovely lady in black," said Kem, as he began to perform one of his hit songs, *When Love Calls*. Lance turned toward me, exhibiting great skill at trying not to turn red, or shall I say, more red, if that was even possible.

I grabbed his left hand, gesturing to him that I wanted to dance. He tried to pull his hand away from me, out of anger, but I held on tight. I figured that if it was going to be Lance that I laid with tonight, I might as well make the most of it. I was so tired of arguing. I just wanted to detach my emotions from my body and just have sex, wild animal-like sex, as men do.

If I got my way, Lance was truly going to be a happy camper, so I made him a proposition that he could not refuse. I started talking dirty in his ear, proposed hot, steamy, rugged sex with no foreplay. Next thing I knew we were at home humping each other like two dogs in heat. I must admit, I enjoyed it more than I thought I would. Lance enjoyed himself, too. He didn't hug, kiss, or caress me. He did just what I told him he could do, have his way with me. He pulled my long curly hair, made me scream all kinds of weird things, and spanked me as if I had brought home all F's on my report card. It was well worth missing the main attraction at the park, the fireworks.

Lance served me one of his succulent veggie omelets and sliced raisin toast breakfasts' in bed. I guess sex does help make you forget how much you despise a person, at least temporarily anyway; well, sex, and the morning after omelet. That's why I kept going back repeatedly. It was the little thoughtful things that Lance did that allowed me to forget all about the little insignificant crisis' he put me through. There I was, wrapped up tightly in his love like a nice cozy blanket on a winter's night once again; until the next set of annoying events occurred.

I must admit I love Lance. Nobody said marriage was going to be easy. I guess I was just tired. I was tired of the same ole', same ole', a monotonous routine that just never quit.

I resented the fact, though, that Lance and I wasted an entire night being angry at each other, just to wake up happily in each other's arms. I know it all started with the Johnny incident so I guess I have Johnny to thank for that. "Thanks Johnny, you jerk."

# Chapter 3

When Lance and I first met almost exactly three years ago, he swept me off my feet. We met at the French Quarter Festival. Lance had on an obviously expensive white linen outfit. I thought I had died and gone to heaven when I first saw him. He looked like an angel. He stuck out like a sore thumb because most people don't dress up for this event. He didn't notice me right away, though. Kayla and I were together, and we were not standing in the most conspicuous place for Lance to notice me. I watched his every move hoping he would look my way, to no avail. I stuffed the last bit of my beignet in my mouth and discreetly told Kayla that I wanted to walk around a little bit. She was open for anything. Kayla, although not the most well put- together female, five-three, one hundred seventy-five pounds with pixy-short natural sandy-brown hair has always been a good sport.

We moved to a spot next to a couple of drunken tourist boys where Lance was more visible. Kayla was talking to me about her bowels being clogged up from all of the crawfish etoufee' she had eaten. I heard her, but I didn't hear her. I was focused on my target and scheming on how I was going to catch his eye. I didn't want to come across as desperate. Kayla and I eased our way over to where Lance and his co-worker Johnny were standing. Johnny noticed us first. He looked at me, turned away, and then did a quick double take. Kayla finally caught on to what was going on. I wanted to get all of my moves in strategic order before I presumptuously alerted her of my plan, which seemed to be executing itself. Johnny started giving me his sexy eye. He even winked once, but he didn't have a thing on Lance, as far as I was concerned. I didn't want to let on that I was disinterested in Johnny right away. That could have messed things up with Lance. I told Kayla to flirt with Johnny to entice them to come over. She was smart, funny, enterprising, and down to earth. Her joyous personality would light up a room. She was aware of it and accepted it for what it was. Kayla embraced who she was and she loved herself, which was most important. She knew she had many good qualities. She said what she lacked in the look's department, God made up for in the intelligence department. Those smarts landed her a 4.0 GPA from Tulane University. She chose a career in law and secured a job at a reputable firm, making six figures. She drove a champagne colored convertible Mercedes Coupe, had a house on St. Charles Avenue, and a lot of other land and assets. Yet, she's so humble. You would never know Kayla had it going on like that. She didn't wear much makeup. No fancy hairstyles nail jobs or sexy outfits. That's just Kayla, got to love her!

She tried the subtle approach to getting Johnny to notice her, but he didn't make any moves. It was not her style to be subtle, anyway. She walked up to Johnny, who smelled as if he had bathed in his cheap cologne, and started talking.

"Hello gentlemen, I'm Kayla and this is my girl Reina," she said, standing close to Johnny, indicating to Lance that he was to talk to me.

I was so embarrassed. All the same, I quickly got over the embarrassment. Lance had no choice but to engage me in a conversation. Kayla made sure of that.

"Well hello Reina, it's a pleasure to meet you."

"Same here," I said, cheesing.

"Are you enjoying yourself?"

"Very much, thank you; how about you?"

"Oh, the food is great but I'm not one for crowds."

"Me either," We chuckled.

During the dry conversation between Johnny and Kayla, Johnny's eyes kept swaying over toward me.

Lance and I exchanged information after a few short minutes of conversation. I looked down at the business card he handed me, noticing he put his home phone number on the back. I was impressed. What woman wouldn't be? Afterwards, I put him through a very extensive examination. In ten minutes, I found out his religion, criminal background, credit history, blood type, sexual orientation, marital status, and his HIV results. I must say that I was mesmerized at how cooperative Lance was, divulging all of that personal information to a complete stranger. Besides, who knows if he was even telling the truth, but at least he humored me. I liked that a lot. We got a big laugh out of it; so much, I did not want to leave. I literally had to pry myself away from him, because I had a strong urge to jump his bones right then and there. It took everything in me to fight the enthusiastic sexual desires that had ignited my libido. I watched intently as his lips moved, while he mellifluously spoke every single word. I had to get to know him better. He could be the one. Kayla did a good job of entertaining Johnny so that Lance and I could focus on one another. I owe her big time for being so assertive. I could see Johnny looking at me from the corner of my eye. He was undoubtedly checking me out. Couldn't he see that I was interested in his friend? I deliberately refrained from giving him any eye contact or any other signals that could be misconstrued. Kayla didn't seem to care that Johnny wasn't giving her much attention. Kayla had a man, anyway. She was just committed to doing her girl a favor. She just kept on talking about any and everything.

"So Johnny do you have any kids?" Kayla pried.

"Kids, Hell no," Johnny said, folding his arms.

"Why do you say it like that, you don't like kids or something?"

"Nope, I'm a player baby," Johnny adamantly expressed.

"Oh wow. Excuse me. At least you're honest," Kayla shook her head and chucked.

Johnny gave Kayla one-word answers while trying to intervene on Lance and my conversation, but we were not easily distracted.

"You better tell'em how we do it," Johnny said excitedly, nudging Lance and rubbing his hands together.

"Hey man, don't include me in on that one. That's all you man, all you."

"Oh so it's like that bruh?"

"Yep, I'm afraid it's like that," Lance immediately turned back toward me.

Johnny got silent and became rude with Lance. He decided all of a sudden that he was ready to leave.

"Let's bounce," Johnny said, sternly.

Everybody else was having a good time, even Kayla, and she could care less. Johnny resented the fact that he didn't have that Creole complexion, blondish-brown-wavy hair, green eyes and dimpled smile that stimulated me and I'm sure lots of other women into an erotic state of bliss from just looking at his boy.

Kayla and I sometimes went through similar situations where a man wanted to meet me and not her, but she didn't get an attitude with me like Johnny did with Lance. I can truly say one thing about my girl Kayla; she was very secure within herself. Had it been me in her shoes, I would be holding my head down, licking my wounds. Thank God for a friend like Kayla. I know many girlfriends that are ensconced in competition with one another. The good Lord knows I have certainly had my share of those kinds of friends, or shall I say acquaintances, before I became wiser.

"Hope to hear from you soon, Reina."

"You will," I smiled, walking away.

Kayla and I walked around from bar to bar, even some gay ones, and devoured a couple of drinks. I was excited about my new friend. I couldn't stop thinking of ways to bag him. I went back and forth with myself, trying to decide which approach I would use on him. He's lucky that I'm not the same little country girl I used to be because back then, I would have taken a very different approach. As I contemplated, I decided that I did not want to throw him the goods. He didn't strike me as the kind of guy that would take kindly to it "coming too easily." I felt like I needed to break out my Merriam-Webster dictionary and brush up on my vocabulary to impress this man. Oh, how I loved a good challenge. This brother needed to be mentally stimulated. He was not your average "look at your breasts while having a conversation with you" brother that I was used to dealing with. In fact, I couldn't recall him looking at them at all; I think I remember this because I had on my favorite Victoria's Secret push up bra. He had every opportunity to indulge his gorgeous eyes at the target, but he didn't. That's how you know a man has class.

Kayla must have drunk at least three Hurricanes before she decelerated her pace. She was talking crazy and slurring her words. I decided that it was time to go home.

Before we could even make it to the car over by the French Market, two young guys walked up and started talking to us. Kayla answered a few of their questions. You know the usual. "Ya'll from around here?" What are your names?" "Can we take ya'll out to dinner?" They said they drove down from Mobile, Alabama.

I tried to walk faster, hoping to lose them somewhere in my dust, but they accelerated their speed to keep up. I couldn't understand how they didn't notice my somewhat rude body language. Some guys just don't care that you clearly don't want to talk to them. I guess they figured if they talked long enough, they would eventually wear us down. I was very short in answering their questions. Since Kayla was friendlier, they evidently felt they were welcomed to continue walking with us. When we got to the car, Kayla clicked the alarm button to unlock the doors to the coupe. I got in on the passenger side, waiting for her to finish up. I didn't want to rush her, especially after she displayed such patience with me at the festival, so I just waited. She ended up talking to the youngsters for about fifteen minutes. I don't know what she was saying, but she sure had their undivided attention. I laid my head back on the plush camel-colored headrest and closed my eyes until I heard the car crank up. I did not ask her what they talked about. I didn't care. All I wanted to do was go home, wait by the phone until Lance called.

I had hoped it wouldn't be another one of those typical guy lines; "I'll call you" and they don't. I was so tired of getting played. I wanted a serious, meaningful relationship, a man of substance, a man with class. I wanted to go on a real date, dinner, and then coffee. A walk along a body of water would even be nice. I wanted to go somewhere quaint with atmosphere and ambiance where we could talk and get to know each other, like they do in the movies. I wanted to talk about important issues and matters of the heart, not your usual boring, frothy conversations, like what they did with their homeboys last night at the club. I did not want a date where his entire suggestion was to pick up a six-pack, go to his apartment and watch a stupid action movie. Soon after, his hands end up under my skirt. That was not a real date, but a booty call. God knows I have had my share of those, but I wanted more.

I wanted a man who had different talents, like . . . I don't know . . . playing the piano . . . or cooking . . . maybe a second language, just something besides playing street ball or X-Box, with his nephews. I was so tired of dating guys whose whole idea of fun was picking up a forty and taking a ride, while stopping off by his different partner's houses dropping off suspicious packages.

Kayla dropped me off at home. I checked messages, hoping Lance's charming voice was on it, but it wasn't. Then it dawned on me, "The three-day rule." The intangible dating rulebook states that one was to wait approximately three days to call a potential romantic interest, so that one does not seem desperate. I had almost forgotten about that, although I didn't want to be the first one to call him either.

I ran a hot, aromatherapy bubble bath and soaked for about an hour. I read the final chapters of Juanita Bynum's, "No more sheets." I figured I needed to put on the whole armor of God to keep me from doing what I was planning on doing to Lance. I had to repent in advance, due to the premeditated acts I was sure I was going to commit. I got on my knees to say a prayer and before I could get a word out, the phone rang. See, that's just how the enemy will come to attack you, when you're trying to do the right thing. That dirty, rotten enemy knew I didn't want to miss the phone call that I had so diligently been waiting for. I hate to say it, but I put my prayer on hold and answered the phone, hoping it was Lance and sure enough, it was.

"Hello," I answered cheerfully.

"Hello, may I speak to Reina please?"

"This is Reina."

"Hi Reina, this is Lance...from the festiv..."

"I know who you are Lance. I didn't forget about you that quickly."

"Oh, well that's good to know. How are you this evening?"

"I'm fine, just a little worn out from earlier."

"I hear you, me too."

"Is your friend Johnny feeling any better, he seemed agitated?"

"I have no idea. He went left and I went right. Good thing we drove separately," he laughed.

"Yeah, I guess so," I chuckled along with him.

"I have a question for you Reina."

"Okay, what is it?"

"Why does someone as beautiful as you not have someone special in your life, or am I being presumptuous?"

"No you aren't. I guess I'm too picky."

"Well that's good for me then. You are absolutely astonishing."

"And you have just earned yourself ten brownie points for all the complements."

"Oh you like that huh? How many do I need total?"

"Uh, about three hundred,"

"Three hundred, wow, I better get on the ball then, huh?"

We talked for three hours straight. We both agreed that we felt a connection and wanted to continue the pursuit of each other. The attraction we shared was obvious, not just to us, but to everyone we encountered. I was impressed that Lance didn't feel compelled to stand firm on the three-day rule. Who made up that stupid rule anyway, why squander away our three days, when we could be spending them together?

Lance and I have not been apart since our first date. We were inseparable, like Bonnie and Clyde.

The lease on my apartment was up, so I moved into his contemporary Condo in the Garden District. Lance struggled daily with celibacy issues. He would lie there, cuddling me until I fell asleep. I woke up on several occasions to find him asleep on the sofa in the living room. He found it hard to sleep in the same bed with me, so we got married after only six months and that's when it all started to go downhill.

# Chapter 4

Rose, my five-pound pet Chihuahua, and I patiently awaited Lance's arrival so we could take a relaxing ride through the French Quarters, to see the tourist attractions. Sometimes we would act as if we were tourists ourselves. We liked to ride the horse and buggies. We would also watch the break dance performances on the steps of Jackson Square while drinking coffee and eating beignets. Sundays were great for a spontaneous ride through the city, stopping to view the art galleries and antique shops. We even had our palms read and the oil painting of ourselves that hung above our bed, we had painted there. When we got hungry, we would stop at a couple of hole-in-the-wall places to have appetizers and a drink or two along the way. I looked forward to our Sundays, since it seemed like the rest of the week belonged to everyone else in his family.

Three o'clock snuck around and Lance was still not home. I didn't realize how fast time had flown by, because I was preoccupied with the lifetime channel. When I noticed the time, I reached for the cordless phone that sat on the end table by the sofa, to call him on his cell. He had gone to church with his mother this morning since I overslept, due to the late hours I kept last night reminiscing with Kayla and Gina on a three-way call about the good old days that really were not that long ago.

I dialed Lance's number to see what was taking him so long to pick me up. We had already lost half of the day and I had a taste for some raw oysters on the half shell. The voice on the other end immediately shifted my mood.

"Hello," Ms. Pearl answered.

It took all of my strength not to scream, so I gritted my teeth in agitation. Lance was still at his mama's house at three o'clock in the afternoon and church had been over since eleven. They went to the nine a.m. service over at Life Center to hear Pastor Wiley preach one of his uplifting sermons.

Today was supposed to be my day. I sucked it up as best I could and let out a shallow, "Hello Ms. Pearl, may I speak to Lance please?"

"Uh-uh, he's busy right now; can I tell him whose calling?" She ignorantly asked, as if she didn't know it was me.

"Ms. Pearl, this is Reina, Lance's wife. I really need to speak to L...."

"Oh, Reina, he's busy right now. I'll tell him you called though."

"It's important that I speak to him now Ms. Pear . . .

"I'll be sure to give him the message. Okay bye, bye," "Click"!

"Wait a min . . ."

That witch hung up on me! I had a good mind to take a high-speed ride over there, but I knew Lance would have a fit if I went to his mama's iron clad house starting a ruckus. Lance said we must respect our elders no matter how irrational they act. I couldn't believe I put up with this crap for three whole years. I wanted a man that was willing to defend my honor, even if it meant standing up to his mama. I wanted him to put me first and dare anybody to treat me unfairly. His mama just kept pushing my buttons and disrespecting me. She callously disregarded my title as Lance's wife. That obviously didn't mean squat to her. I know one thing, I am sick of her. At that moment, I thought to myself that if she kept messing with me, she had better watch her back. At this point in my life, what do I really have to lose, a husband who was never home anyway, so what? I was over it. I needed to vent so I called Kayla before I exploded.

"Hello," answered Kayla.

"Hey girl," I said, depressed.

"Reina, girl what's wrong?"

"I am sick to death of Lance's mama. I don't know what to do."

"What happened this time?" Kayla sounded unsurprised.

"Girl, I have been waiting for Lance to come home since early this morning so we could go riding and spend some quality time together; at three o clock, no Lance. I called his cell phone and Ms. Pearl's crazy ass answers. She pretends not to know who I am, refuses to call him to the phone, then hangs up in my face; How about that, huh?"

"How rude," Kayla said, sounding as if she were frowning!

"That's what I'm saying. She could've called him to the phone."

"Wanna go over there?"

"Yep, but I know Lance would act a fool on me, for disrespecting his mama's house."

"Don't disrespect her house, just go get your man and bring him home!"

"How, drag him by his ears?"

"Reina think, sweetie. What is the only language that men understand?"

"Uh . . ."

"Girl, you taking too long, I'll give you a hint. It starts with a P."

"P?"

"Look, just go put on some skin tight daisy dukes and a low-cut halter, go over there, ring the bell and sit in the driveway on the hood of your car and... vogue or something."

"Vogue,"

"Reina, don't you remember anything Madonna taught us?"

"Girl, you so crazy,"

"Yeah, that's true, but I guarantee my man would much rather watch me model for him rather than looking at his old ass mama."

"You got a point there, girl."

"Then it's settled. Oh, and don't forget to wear your favorite push up bra. That's how you caught him in the first place, remember?"

"Well, I never actually caught him looking at them, and besides, he would never admit it, anyway."

"That's the beauty of being a woman, sweetie. He doesn't have to, but we both know the deal."

"You are too much Kayla, but you're right."

"Thanks. Call me when the madness is over. I'm anxious to see how everything fares out," Kayla said.

"You got it, girl. I let you buck me up again. You got me going over to this woman's house, half naked, like I'm going to steal him from his mistress."

"Well Reina, you have a mama's boy on your hands. She lures him over there with her fried chicken, jambalaya, cabbage, homemade cornbread, okra gumbo, and sweet potato pie, from scratch, I might add. So that means that you have to lure him back home with your . . . your . . . well whatever you're planning to lure him with. I don't even want to know what that is, and call it even," Kayla laughed aloud.

"You know what it is girlfriend. It's all of these feminine wiles I was blessed with, don't hate."

"Yeah, that must be it, uh huh," Kayla patronizingly teased.

"You know that's it."

Anyway, call me later after the smoke clears!"

"Alright Kay girl, bye,"

"Bye."

Rose sat close to my feet staring at me with her large round, very dark ruby eyes as if she were anxious to put on her Sunday dress and go out as well. I put on her body harness and took her on a brief walk.

Why did I continue to listen to Kayla? I really didn't think I would feel comfortable going over to his mother's house in a skimpy pair of shorts, strutting around for the whole neighborhood to see. I could see that plan backfiring on me. I didn't think he would appreciate my shenanigans. If anything, he would yell at me for showing off what he called my goodies, to the whole neighborhood. Lance was very jealous, so I thought I ought to pass on Kayla's idea. I just did as I always did . . . wait for him to come home, we'd argue, he'd leave, I'd watch some more television, then, it was lights out for me, as usual.

On the other hand, if I did not make a stink about him coming home late, then he would come home with a dozen red, long-stemmed roses and a long, drawn-out story about what kept him so long. "I apologize," he would say. So, let me weigh my options. Did I want to make a stink to let him know how I felt about him breaking our plans or do I opt for the roses and the sorry poor apology, hmmm? I chose to make the stink. I was tired of something always coming up. I knew he was an Aquarius, but Lord knows if I had known then what I know now, I would not have been contemplating half of the things that I was contemplating, like leaving his sorry butt. Ugh, I was really looking forward to that ride.

I always tried to abide by the "rules." I allowed Lance to be the leader of our home, even if it meant putting my dreams on hold for a little while. I tried to see things his way to keep the peace and make him feel like "the man." I needed him to feel good about us, so I permitted him to make most of the decisions in our relationship, so he could shine. He had always proven himself quite an astute businessperson at work, so I felt confident that he would do the same at home. Even if he made a decision that I didn't agree with, I would not undermine him. However, three years of standing by my man, while he sat by me, had finally overwhelmed me. I no longer possessed the capacity to continue in the relationship based on the way my feelings teetered back and forth.

Rose and I returned from our walk, around the entire complex. She was so tired that she went straight to her designer canopy doggie bed I bought her for Christmas last year, to lie down.

Hours passed by, no Lance. I looked at the cable directory to view the time... seven thirty pm.

"Well, he did it again," I thought.

I decided not to say a word about it, after all. I just allowed myself to fall deeper and deeper out of love every time he did something wrong, so I would have a reason to feel good about leaving. I did not want to end my marriage that I tenaciously held on to for three years but I didn't feel I had a choice. I needed a man who wanted to spend his spare time with me.

I heard the keys jingle in the keyhole. I slid down deeper into our leather sofa cushion to give the appearance that I had been home relaxing and not thinking about him, although I felt sickened by the anticipation of his return home. I was infuriated, but I could not bring myself to give him the pleasure of knowing how hurt and angry I was. Hell would have to freeze over this time before I let him know that he bruised my ego black and blue. Usually I would whine and cry when I didn't get my way, because he tended to respond better to tears. My plan was to be strong. I would just sit quietly, listening to what he had to say, if it killed me. Oh God, I had hoped it wouldn't kill me. In return, I would kill him, with kindness. I learned that little trick from my adopted mother. She was always kind to everyone even if they were undeserving of it. That's what I did. I reincarnated myself into my mother and prayed I was able to endure, without going off on him.

"Honey, I'm home," Lance said as he entered the house, doing his Ricky Ricardo impersonation.

"Hey," I said dryly, continuing to watch TV.

"Sorry I'm a little late, boo; Mom told me you called, but I was in the middle of painting her bedroom," explaining the situation.

"Uh huh, that's nice," I responded, condescendingly.

"So, you still want to take that ride, gorgeous? We can go to our favorite spot on the river and do a little smooching, if you want, but don't let me twist your arm," Lance flirted.

"Did he not get it, or what?" I thought to myself.

"Oh, no that's okay Lance. I'm kind of tired and I've gotten into this good movie."

"You sure babe, it's not too late? We still have a couple of daylight hours left. I'll even buy you a hurricane from Pat O Brian's, just let me take a shower and throw on something debonair for you. You'll change your mind," he continued, hurrying.

He made it almost impossible for me to stay mad at him. He could be so sweet, but I had to stand my ground or else he would walk all over me.

"No thanks," never tearing my eyes away from the TV.

"Okay then, sweetheart, suit yourself. I'm going to take a shower. See you when I get out."

"Okay," nodding nonchalantly, trying my best to stay angry.

Lance walked into the bathroom and started running the water. He always ran the water for about five minutes before he actually got in the shower. I had no idea why, but it annoyed me. Lance walked out of the bathroom into the bedroom to get his boxer briefs, then back to the bathroom, naked. That man was so fine, but, as fine as he was, I could not see past my anger.

While Lance showered, I called Gina to see if she wanted some company for the weekend, in the Big Apple. I needed to get away and clear my head. The more I thought about it, the more I embraced the idea of going away to get my party on. Gina was the perfect remedy.

# Chapter 5

The newscaster predicted an eighty percent chance of rain for the evening and I was unprepared for it. I had forgotten my black leather jacket in the airport, left my umbrella in Louisiana and the last raincoat I owned was when I was about six years old. It was bright yellow. My adopted grandmother on my father's side, Whila Mae bought it for me, rest her soul.

Flights to New York were always frustrating to me. The last time I had flown, I will never forget, I had an aisle seat, 18C. It seemed like everyone had to use the toilet at the same time. People kept bumping my seat. A little kid with an oblivious mother sat behind me and repeatedly kicked the back of my chair. I became infuriated, but I wasn't sure if I was angry with the little girl or her mother. This time, I sat next to a heavy-set man whose thighs spilled over into my seat. He reeked of alcohol and fell fast asleep before the plane left the ground. He snored loudly and his head kept sliding in my direction. I spent the entire flight anticipating the fall; between that and his gurgling snores, I didn't know which was worse. I asked the flight attendant if there were any other seats available anywhere else on the plane. She looked at me, then at the man with the scruffy salt and pepper beard to my right, and smiled. She went to "see what she could do." Later, she came back and said "unfortunately, there weren't any". The plane was one hundred percent full, as always, going to New York. They overbooked the flight, as usual and gave us the opportunity to give up our seat for compensation. I was tempted but I declined. I was ready to get to my destination. The bright side was that I enjoyed sitting next to the window fading into the clouds, while snacking on my complementary bag of Chex-mix and sipping on a miniature bottle of tanqueray.

Gina and I had only seen each other a couple of times since our college days, but we talked all of the time. We had a great time living together back then. After talking it over with my parents, we decided it would probably be a better choice for me to attend Xavier University to finish my Sociology degree. This time, they urged me to live on campus, instead of having my own apartment, like in Baton Rouge. I didn't get much studying done living with Gina. She had me at somebody's keg or toga party every weekend, and sometimes during the week. When I moved to New Orleans, she went back to Jersey for a while. We couldn't stand being away from each other. I convinced her to enroll at Xavier as well; she eventually did. Since she got her degree in finance, she is back in the Big Apple, living in Brooklyn where she always said she would. She wanted to be closer to her mother. She bought a brownstone and that's where I stayed.

I stood outside of LaGuardia Airport trying to flag a taxi. Everyone I flagged seemed to be full of passengers. I missed having Rose with me. She was my little travel companion, but I knew that she would have barked at all of the passersby on the plane, so I left her in Lance's custody for the weekend. A cute little Puerto Rican fellow offered to help me with my bags, but I refused. He was too flirty. I didn't feel up to indulging in meaningless chitchat. I was on a mission to get to Gina's house so we could catch up on old times. Gina was my dearest friend. I had known her a little longer than I had Kayla, although we were all close; that was the extent of my circle. I didn't need any more friends. Having those two in my life was quite enough for one person to handle.

I was finally able to get a taxi, hopped in and headed toward Gina's humble abode.

"Girl, I thought you'd never get here," she said, hugging my neck as tightly as she could.

"Gina, I can't breathe," I said, as we both burst into laughter.

"It's so good to see you, Reina Ann Joseph."

"Oh, you had to go there, calling out my full name, huh, Ms. Gina Lorraine Scott?

We were so happy to see each other. We couldn't stop belly laughing. We were like tobacco and spit, but now like peas and carrots, separate, but still go good together. We shared many memories together, good, and bad.

"How your mama nem, Gee?"

"Ha, girl you know you from New Orleans, huh? That tramp aight, still sucking on her suds every night. I can see her now; ninety-five years old still calling for me to grab her beer out of the Frigidaire, as she calls it."

"Oh my God," I laughed.

"Girl it wouldn't even matter if she had teeth, as long as she had a hole in her throat, she'll still be sucking down those beers."

"Now, why are you talking about Mama Lee like that? You leave Leona alone; let her suck on her beers if she wants to! Nah," I giggled.

"Yeah, yeah, whatever, chick,"

The grin on her face made me realize how much I had missed her.

"Come on, let's unpack your things!"

"Wow, how fun," I returned, ducking Gina's playful punch."

"I want to go see all of the fine men you've been telling me about."

"Don't worry, there are plenty of them around here to keep us busy your whole trip, trust me," Gina said, looking at me with a grin on her face. "As a matter of fact, some fool down at the subway handed me a flyer saying something about a party tonight. I didn't even read it, but its right behind you on the bed."

I picked up the flyer, it read:

"All you party people show your face in the place, for the baddest, wham bam, thank you ma'am Record Release Party, featuring Lyrical Record's latest rap duo, Rowdy Red and Gangsta Slim. Come out and show your love."

"Girl, this party is going to be off the hook. Rowdy Red and Gangsta Slim are having their record release party tonight," I said, excitedly.

"Who?"

"Rowdy Red and Gangsta Slim;"

"Reina, you actually know who they are?"

"I've heard of them from Kayla. You know she keeps up with the latest music."

"Girl, you know I don't do the gangster rap thing."

"Yeah, I know me either. I feel like doing something crazy though."

"Like what?"

"I'm not sure exactly. Let's just go and see what happens."

"Are you sure girl? What if they start shooting?"

"The least we can do is go down and check it out. If we feel the slightest bit uncomfortable, we can leave, okay?"

"Alright Reina, it's your vacation, we'll do whatever you want to do. I'm just glad you're here."

"Me too, I'm so excited. I haven't been anywhere in a long time."

"Well, you can come visit me anytime you want to."

"Oh... thank you Gee, I might have to take you up on that."

"Why, you trying to get away from Lance?" Gina said, laughing.

For the first time since Gina and I laid eyes on each other, the room was silent.

"Reina, you okay? Did I say something wrong?"

"I think I'm going to leave him, Gee."

"What?"

"You heard me right."

"Okay . . . but . . . are you guys having problems?"

"Girl, do you mind if we talk about this later? I don't want to start thinking about Lance. It'll just make me get angry."

"Okay, anything you want. How about we grab a latte and walk around the village for a while?"

"That sounds good. Let's go."

"Are you ready, girl," asked Gina, egging me on?

"I couldn't be any more ready, so put one foot in front of the other and lead the way."

Gina and I headed toward the village. We hopped on the subway. We had to stand up for most of the ride and what a bumpy ride it was. I think our driver was tipsy, because the train bucked back and forth during the take off. I don't know what it is about public transportation and me, but that was also one of the strangest experiences of my life. There are weird people in New Orleans, for sure, but New York took the cake. There was a tall, lanky man with long, stringy hair standing next to us having an entire conversation with himself; he even did a few "brick wall" gestures, with his hands to his own face.

A few feet from him stood a trio, singing old Prince Songs like *nineteen ninety-nine* and playing instruments made out of kitchen utensils. They must have collected at least twenty dollars from the passengers in our car alone. There were a couple of what appeared to be gang bangers, sitting side by side, throwing hand signals at each other. This might be a stretch, but I don't think they were deaf. They were both wearing blue bandanas that knotted to the left, overly baggy jeans and tennis shoes that were untied.

Lastly, I involuntarily entered a staring contest with a disheveled Caucasian homeless woman. She could not take her eyes off me. She sat quietly in her seat wearing old, torn, ragged clothing, holding a couple of worn bags on her lap. I felt bad. I wanted to give her a few dollars, but Gina said no, it would not be a good idea, because then we would look vulnerable, others would start asking too. My heart went out to her and I felt like I should have been doing something to help her, but I didn't know what. Maybe some food . . . money . . . a hot shower, I didn't know. Gina suggested we just say a prayer for her, so I discreetly bowed my head.

As I sat in my seat, I couldn't help thinking about how hospitable it was down south where I was from. When people needed help, we were there to extend a helping hand, unlike New York, where everyone who was not engaging in some sort of dysfunctional activity stayed to themselves. In the south people say, "Good morning," and have idle chit chat with you. Not to mention where both of my grandmas' Whila Mae and Big Mama were from, deep down in Southern Mississippi. If you walked by someone's house, you had better have enough sense to speak to them. Everybody knew everybody in the country parts. If they caught you doing something wrong, they would beat you, tell your parents, then your parents would beat you again. When it was all over, they would feed you.

Every Sunday felt like Thanksgiving. Whila Mae would cook cabbage, ham hocks, black-eyed peas, chitterlings, cornbread dressing, and all kinds of cakes and pies. All of the church members would take turns going to each other's houses to feast, and then take a nap before the evening services started. Ole' Grandma Whila Mae was the church Mother. I know I must have eaten at just about everybody's house in Woodville, at some point.

Big Mama could not cook so much anymore, after she had gotten sick with uterine cancer. Grandma Whila Mae gladly took on the sole responsibility of making sure the whole family was country cornbread fed every Sunday.

I was glad to be back on the ground where I felt I had the most control. I loved to be entertained, but the subway ride was a bit much, even for me. I was so anxious to see the Big Apple, at last.

"Let's go in here, Gee. This looks like a fun place."

The Snake Pit was located down in the heart of the east village.

"The Snake Pit, ugh, sounds kind of grungy if you ask me."

"Well I'm not asking you. I'm putting my foot down girl."

"Alright, you're responsible for my blood on your hands when one of these big burly bikers hauls us into the back alley and slices us into pieces, okay?"

"You have the most colorful imagination I've ever seen Gee. And anyway, when did you become so uppity?"

"A couple of years ago when I realized, I wasn't poor anymore," Gina said, laughing.

"Well don't forget the good old days, when we lived together and ate smashed vienna sausage sandwiches for dinner."

"How could I forget those days? We really lived it up back then, huh? It didn't matter if we had money or not. No one cared, because we were in college; nobody had any money. Now, it matters, trust me! In the real world, it takes money to make money. Nobody wants to be bothered with you if you don't have anything to offer them. If you're broke, people won't give you any money, but, if you're broke, but look and act like you have some money, then they'll give you some money. Isn't that interesting?"

"Gina what in the world, are you talking about?"

"Never mind girl. I went off on one of my tangents again."

"I see why you like riding that train with all those crazy people. You fit right in with them."

We laughed, walking past a horde of motorcycles.

"Don't worry about it girl. You don't get me," Gina pushed the swinging double doors.

"Girl, the only thing I'm about to get right now, is a beer," I said sliding into the first open booth with ripped leather seats, closest to the doors in case we had to run out in a jiffy.

"Well you don't think I'm just going to sit here and watch you get your party started without me, do you?"

"Alright girl, that's the spirit."

We looked around and commented to each other on the shabby attributes of the bar; paint chipping from the walls and such. The clientele consisted of a low rate, but diverse crowd. A waitress wearing a wide brim hat, cow-hide vest, a short jean skirt and cowboy boots walked over to our table to take our drink order.

"Two drafts please," said Gina, ordering for us.

Gina always had a take-charge way about her. It didn't bother me any. That was less I had to think of. I liked people who made my life less complicated. Gina had that special gift. Even though I was a year older than her, she always played the mothering role. Gina could hold her own in the party department with the best of them. However, when it came time to take care of business, she was able to find the balance from somewhere. Me? Ah, that was a different story. I was an extremist; passionate about whatever it was I was doing at the time. Whether that was partying or studying. Gina could juggle both at the same time.

"So Reina, outside of the Lance issues, what's been going on with you?"

"Well, I'm still working for Lance's friend's mother's furniture store. I can't believe it's been two years already."

"Oh, I thought you said you were going back into sociology?"

"Well, I was, but Lance keeps telling me to give this furniture thing a real shot first. He convinced me of how well I upholstered furniture. People love my work too. They featured me in the local newspaper for a couple of pieces I had done. We received a ton of business because of that little article. I was flattered. I was having a good hair day that day too. My picture came out so cute. A couple of people on the street even came up to me saying that they saw me in the paper. I didn't know people actually read that stuff."

"So have you decided to make a career of it?"

"I don't know. I don't really like it but apparently I'm good at it."

"Reina, are you happy?" Gina asked, slowly reaching across the small wooden table to hold my hand.

"I don't know."

"Why don't you know, I don't understand?"

"Sometimes I'm really happy, and then sometimes I want to choke him."

"That just sounds like good old-fashioned marriage, to me."

"Really, Gee?

"Yeah girl, from the bits and pieces you've already told me, I've gathered that Lance is sweet, romantic, fine as wine and he pays all the bills. Am I missing anything? Are you listening to yourself?"

"Well when you say it like that, I sound like a selfish, spoiled brat."

"All I'm saying is give your marriage a fair chance. Don't throw your hands up just because things don't go your way all the time. I know you're a diva and all of that, but that man loves you girl. Do you know how many women would love to be in your shoes right now, including me, so you better hold on to that man, hold on tight, nobody's perfect? I had to learn my lesson the hard way."

"What about all the time he spends away from home, helping the entire Joseph family with all of their problems,"

"Reina, is he cheating on you?"

"No!"

"Oh, then he must be beating you, right?"

"Hell no,"

"Girl, we are running out of options here. You better give me something!"

"He knows better than to put his hands on me!"

"Okay girl, no need to start getting all ghetto on me, rolling your eyes and neck at the same time. That's not cute. We've evolved remember?"

Gina was right. I had clicked over to my other personality just that fast, Sheniqwa. She's the neck-rolling, finger-pointing sister part of me that surfaces when I'm in defense mode; although I'm still able to be myself around Gina, since she knew me before my full transformation into Mrs. Lance Joseph.

"I don't know where I would go if I left him anyway. I don't have any money."

"What do you do with all of your money?"

"Spend it. Lance pays all the bills in the house, even my car note. The only things he makes me pay are my credit card bills. He says I have to pay for my own social life and my own habits."

"Well, that sounds fair."

"Yeah, it's cool."

"I just don't want to see you get hurt, since you're so unprepared, in the event of a break up, like the one you are obviously planning."

"You mean, me relying solely on him to take care of me?"

"Exactly, you should think twice about leaving first of all, and secondly, you should always save for a rainy day."

"I know! That's what's so scary about me leaving Lance. He takes care of everything. To be honest with you Gee, I don't know if I still want him or if I just don't want anybody else to have him. Cause when it's good, it's really good."

"Do you see yourself in the mirror yet?"

"I have been really stupid, haven't I?"

"No, you just lost your way for a minute, but you're back on track now," Gina said, relieved.

"I'm so lucky to have you as a friend Gee. You're always saving my butt from a disaster. It's been too long since we've seen each other. I'm so glad I'm here. Thank you. I needed to hear those things. No matter what, you always tell me the truth, even if it hurts a little."

"No problem. I'm glad I could be of assistance," Gina said, smiling.

"I really owe you one this time."

"Oh good, I'm glad you feel that way. You can pay your debt as soon as the cowgirl comes back over here. My glass is empty," Gina bantered.

I suggested we go shake a tail feather. We downed a few drinks while watching the drunken patrons' ride the mechanical bull, then meandered our way to the dance floor. We danced together approximately one minute flat when the guys showing off their hoedown moves and cavity-ridden smiles started coming out of nowhere to dance with us. We didn't want to seem unfriendly, so we didn't brush them off as abruptly as we would have liked to. We did our Miss America wave, as we approached the door after two-stepping to a couple of songs.

"Bye," we said, in unison, as we waved our way out to the street.

"Can you believe it girl, we're still alive," I joked.

"Yeah, yeah, I guess it wasn't that bad, although all of the women in there were lesbian biker chicks. I couldn't tell the guys from the girls, could you?" Gina looked confused.

"Who cares, I had fun. What's our next stop?" I asked, excitedly.

"You are in rare form today, huh?"

"Yes I am, and it's only six o clock. It's still early. I have an idea. Why don't we go surprise Mama Leona?"

"Are you serious? She would love that."

"Of course, I couldn't come all this way and not see my girl. Where does she live?"

"She lives in Brooklyn, not too far from my place."

"Ya'll surely do a lot of traveling back and forth on that train, huh?"

"Yeah, but once you get used to it, it becomes second nature. Let me call her to make sure she's going to be home."

"Girl, Leona gets around good, huh?"

"Well, sometimes her gentleman friend Jimmy picks her up and they go either to the casino or to the Lions Club for bingo."

"Gina, are you telling me Leona has a man?"

"She says they're just friends, but yeah."

"What kind of man, I mean . . . who was he . . . is he cute . . . How old . . ."

"Which question do you want me to answer first girl, dang?"

"Any one of them, just start talking."

"He's a really nice guy, very handsome, fifteen years her junior has two kids, works as a cook down at the . . ."

"Back up!"

"Huh?"

"Fifteen years? Alright Leona," I exclaimed, as I snapped my fingers above my head like the homosexuals do.

"I know. I'm embarrassed about it," Gina mumbled under her breath.

"Why, there's nothing wrong with Stella trying to get her gr . . ."

"Enough already, what was she thinking? She's fifty-four and he's only thirty-nine."

"So, what's wrong with that?"

"I don't know. He might be trying to turn my mama out or something."

"I hate to be the one to break it to you, Gee, but Leona got turned out long ago, trust me. Matter of fact she might be the one turning him out."

"Don't talk about Leona like that," Gina said playfully pulling my hair as we crossed the street. "She's still my mother, even though she acts like she's still twenty-two."

"That's probably what Jimmy like's about her, her wild side," I teased.

Gina called Leona to see if we could go over and visit. They talked a couple of seconds. Leona could not hear what Gina was saying. The slot machines were making too much noise.

"We'll go by and see her tomorrow. She's at the casino, as I suspected."

"Is she with Jimmy?"

"Yep, that's her road dog. She doesn't go anywhere without that man."

"Yes indeed! Jimmy must be putting it down . . . okay, okay. I'm just kidding. I'm sorry girl," I said laughing, as Gina twisted my arm.

"Are you hungry?"

"I could eat. The only food you get in coach are some peanuts and dry Chex-mix, enough to gag somebody."

"How about Italian?"

"Fine by me, you know I'm not picky when it comes to eating. I'll eat just about anything."

"I know this cute little place. I think you'll enjoy it."

"Well, let's go."

Gina brought me to a very exclusive, quaint Italian restaurant that housed maybe ten small tables inside and ten outside on the wrought iron covered patio. The tables were dressed in Irish crème linen tablecloths with lace embroidery on the bottom. It was very small yet eloquent in personality. The food was delectably prepared and the five star services were impeccable. Gina said she had made the reservations over a month ago for her and a date but she took me instead, since I blew into town on such short notice. She knows I like the sensation of the fine dining experience. That was the bourgeois side of my personality and we will just call her Rebecca, Becky for short. Our Italian server, Antonio, was friendly and made us feel right at home from the instant we stepped foot in the family-oriented establishment. He recognized Gina from her eating there once before. He had served her and Leona for Leona's fifty-fourth birthday lunch celebration. Gina explained that I was visiting the city, so on and so forth, so he treated us to a piece of cheesecake for dessert. That was nice of him. The floor was spotless enough to eat from and the walls appeared to be freshly painted. The place in general was immaculate. I was impressed.

"Reina, don't freak out, but when I was walking back from the restroom, the waiter Antonio, asked if he could meet you."

"Are you serious?"

"He's looking this way, don't be so obvious!"

"Gina, you leaning over to me, telling me not to be obvious, is obvious."

"Well, are you going to meet him or not?"

"I hope he doesn't think that I owe him some "thank you coochie" in return for that piece of cheesecake he gave me, huh?"

"Who cares what he thinks, girl? I just want to be entertained.

"Oh really, well in that case, sure, I'll meet him. Send him over!"

Gina merrily beckoned Antonio to come over to our table. He quickly followed her lead as if she were giving him the friends and family hook up.

"Reina, Antonio here has inquired about you. What do you think of that?" Gina said, smiling big, showing off the small gap in between her teeth.

"Well, I'm flattered Antonio. Thank you for your interest, but I'm married," I said, holding out my hand, showing him my flawless two-karat rock.

Gina looked flabbergasted. She thought she was about to have some fun with this little hook up game, but I nipped it in the bud before it even got started. Lance would have been so proud of me.

Hell, I was proud of me, because when I left home and kissed him good-bye, it really felt like goodbye, for me, but thanks to my girl Gina, I was back on track.

"Oh, I'm sorry. I didn't mean to . . ."

"No, it's alright, really. I'm flattered."

"I'm so embarrassed."

"Don't be. It's fine, honest."

"Okay then. You enjoy the rest of your stay here in our city."

"I'm sure I will. Thank you very much."

Antonio walked away holding his head down, with his tail between his legs back to the kitchen. Gina looked at me, perplexed.

"Girl, why did you do that?"

"He wanted to meet me and he did, no problem, right? Anyway, what did you expect me to do, Dear Abby? You're the one who said don't throw your hands up when you don't get your way and give Lance another try?"

"I guess I thought you were just going to play with him a little bit. You just set the poor boy back ten years with that rejection. He really thought he had a chance too."

"Why, what did you tell him, that I was lonely and desperate?"

"No crazy girl, just that you probably wouldn't mind meeting him, especially since I failed to mention the part about you being . . . married."

"I'm going to try to work things out with my husband. I don't need any distractions, because you and I both know how easily I can get caught up. So it's best I leave sexy Antonio alone, trust me."

"You are absolutely right. You are doing the right thing too, girl. Don't let anybody sway you from what's in your heart, not even me. That was those three beers talking, forgive me Reina."

"Gina, I'm not trippin on you. I'm the one that's wishy-washy. I can't make up my mind from one minute to the next, because things keep changing."

"Well, we can still have a grand time without the company of those stinky ole men."

"There you go. You're single; it's okay with me if you want to have some company over. I don't mind. I can amuse myself for a little while."

"I'll keep that in mind, but I'd much rather spend the little bit of time we have together. You're only here a couple of days. Can't you stay for the week? I can take a few sick days."

"Lance didn't want me to come in the first place. He figured you and I together again would be like the old college days. For some reason he thinks I'm easily influenced, but I'm not."

"Well, you've told him so many stories of how I put you up to stuff, it's no wonder he's worried sick," Gina said laughing.

"You do remember what I'm referring to, don't you?"

"Yes, you were always pressuring me to do something crazy, but I'm a different person now. Back then, I guess I was looking for adventure like the rest of the college kids."

"Maybe you should explain that to Lance."

"Do you think I haven't tried?"

"Lance has his own theories. He says birds of a feather flock together, and that's it."

"So he sits around thinking up all kinds of neat clichés' to make you feel guilty, huh?"

"Yeah, you could say that. I think he's just an insecure person, by nature. I can't explain it."

"Generally people do tend to hang around with other people who have the same hobbies or interests as themselves, so I can logically see where he's coming from. He's just going about this all wrong. He has to trust you."

"Try telling him that!"

"Maybe you guys need some counseling. Would he be willing to? ..."

"Hell No,"

"Well I'll just be . . . could I get the rest of the question out first, please?"

"Lance says we don't need a third party in our business."

"Okay, a counselor might seem to him like someone was suggesting that he's a nut. What about his minister?"

"I guess we could talk to Pastor Wiley, but I don't know for sure."

"Oh well. I'm sure you'll figure something out. We've got to get home and get ready if you still want to crash this party tonight."

"I'm ready. You don't have to tell me twice."

Gina and I caught the subway back to her house to prepare for the night's festivities.

# Chapter 6

"Everybody say, OH . . . YEAH . . . , say, OH . . . YEAH . . .," The crowd screamed, as Gangsta Slim's voice echoed through the large crowd. Club Jigga overwhelmed me with its distinct smoky aroma, combined with the stench of old stale liquor, sweaty bodies covered with cheap to expensive perfume and fog machine condensation.

The females walked around the club, flinging their sew-in weaves and looking at each other with competitive eyes. It seemed like they were having a silent contest to see whose skirt was hiked up the highest while "popping their thangs" and "backing it up" on the fellas, as they jumped around bobbing their heads and waving their hands in the air to the funky beats, sounding off from the booming sub woofers.

Gina and I inconspicuously stood by and observed the scene to see how much of our guard we could let down.

"This is a really wild crowd, huh girl?" asked Gina, discreetly looking around at her surroundings, trying not to seem obviously uncomfortable.

"Yeah, but I think it's going to be okay," I said, reassuringly.

"How can you tell?" Gina asked.

"Everyone seems to be having a good time. Besides that, there are at least five or six plain clothed police officers in here," I told her.

"How in the world do you know that, Reina? Gina asked puzzled.

"Oh, I can spot them a mile away. They're just standing around watching everything that goes on. They aren't dancing or drinking. See that guy over there in the corner wearing the blue jeans and Tommy Hilfiger pullover?" I asked, subtly pointing in his direction.

"Oh yeah, I see him," said Gina, moving her head from side to side, trying to get a better view through people's heads.

"He's 5 O! I'll bet you any money, that's water in the cup he's holding. Want to put a little wager on it?" I asked her.

"How are we going to find out what he's drinking?"

"You just leave that up to me. Do you care to indulge me in a friendly little game of Police Detective?" I asked, with my eyebrows raised.

"I really don't think we should be messing with the police, if he is the police," Gina questioned, hesitantly.

"Stop being a scary cat and follow my lead!"

Gee and I slowly crept our way through the crowd, over to where the tall, well-built, nerdy dressed man stood.

"Hi handsome," I blurted out as I stood directly in front of him, smiling a flirtatious smile.

"Hi," he said, smiling a crooked smile back at me, as if he could not believe someone would walk boldly up to him and just start talking.

"Well, how about it? Want to dance with me? This is my song." I asked him, grabbing his free hand into mine to get a reaction.

"I would, but I . . . I can't dance very well," he stuttered.

Hmm, quick on his toes, I thought.

"Well, this round is on me. What are you drinking?" I asked, while signaling to the bartender.

"I don't drink," he said, looking down nervously at his cup hoping his cover wasn't about to be blown.

Gina and I looked at each other in silence, trying to penetrate through his mysterious façade without giving ourselves away.

"Okay then, it was nice meeting you anyway . . . I'm Reina, by the way." I said, pretending to be disappointed from his rejection.

"I'm Alexander. You girls have fun tonight. Be safe!" He said, short, but sweetly, almost shoving us away.

"Okay, and don't you over do it on the fun." I responded, sarcastically, while grabbing Gee by the arm and walking away.

Gina and I found an open spot in the crowd that lasted, all of a minute, to chat about Alexander.

"Girl you were right. That dude was either a cop or gay," Gina said, shaking her head laughing.

"I told you. Could they be any more obvious?" I asked her.

"Okay, okay, you win. What do I owe you?" Gina asked, playfully disgusted. She was sure she was going to win the bet.

"Let me think about it for a while. I'm sure I'll come up with something really interesting,"

"How about I just buy your next drink?" Gina asked, sure of herself.

"No, that's too easy," we both chuckled.

The new generation hip-hop crowd grew larger as the night went on. By this time, Rowdy Red had taken off his shirt to show off that bony rib cage of his, but nobody seemed to care. The vulgar and offensive rap lyrics protruded through the airwaves, straight to our ears. It seemed though, the more vulgar the rap, the rowdier the bling-bling wearing, would be gun toting if they weren't frisked at the door, thugs behaved and the harder the women shook themselves.

This one chick, with long micro-braided extensions dirty danced and rolled her big, apple bottom booty (as the guys would call it) that she squeezed into a plaid tennis skirt, on just about every bugaboo in the place. She was so inebriated that she didn't even notice her tiny miniskirt was hiked up to her bellybutton. Gina wanted to tell her, but she didn't want any trouble from the dudes, who seemed to be having too much fun at her expense.

Gina and I stood on the sidelines, watching in disbelief, along with some of the other patrons in the audience. The female spectacle bent over forward, put her hands on the dirty concrete ground, and rolled her tattooed buttocks that read, "Doodie was here" up and down to the beat of the music, against this one particular guy's swelling bulge. He wrapped his large fingers tightly around her thick bottom half that spread wider the lower she bent. He pointed himself toward her then motioned a sign of elation to his boys. She had to be a stripper by trade, because part of the limber moves that she per-formed required ample skill. When she realized she had the entire audience intently watching her, she added a couple of extra lewd moves to her routine. My favorite one that I planned on secretly practicing for Lance, was, when she bent over forward, grabbed the heels of her six inch, thigh high, spiked boots, looked up at the guy through her legs, made one booty cheek bounce at a time, then gently shook herself into a frenzy. That was the bomb, if I must say so myself.

Rowdy Red and Gangsta Slim lost the undivided attention of their fans due to the strip tease the fellas on the dance floor were getting.

"Are you ready to go yet?" asked Gina, disgustedly.

"Well, not really. It's just starting to get interesting in here. You ready to go already, girl?" I asked her.

"I just can't stand watching this sister degrade herself this way. I'm so disappointed," said Gina, shaking her head in disapproval.

"She knows exactly what she's doing. When she saw that she had spectators, she went wild. Some chicks like that kind of attention,"

"Yeah, but what does that say about us as African American wom-en, Reina? You have to look at the bigger picture,"

"What does it say?

"It subconsciously sends the signal to the men, that all black women must like negative attention. If you want to know why we're not fully respected as Nubian queens, it's because of what we did to that guy at the gas station in Mississippi some years ago and this sister here doing her raunchy version of the Harlem Shake. She's setting us back further and further with every one of her booty claps. I guarantee it. Somebody needs to talk to her," said Gina.

"You can't save the world, Gina, especially at a night club during a record release party." I said, trying to convince her to chill out and just have some fun.

"I don't want to save the world Reina, just this sister right now. I've learned from my mistakes in the past. There could be another officer friendly out there somewhere right now just watching her and waiting for his chance. You do remember the police officer, don't you? Well me, personally, I will never forget it as long as I live."

"So what do you plan to say to her? Don't expect me to mess up my fresh French manicure when she tries to kick your butt for interrupting her groove," I told her.

"It won't come to that. I can be very tactful when I need to be. I just usually don't use any of it on you. You're my girl. I shouldn't have to," said Gina.

"okay, if you really feel compelled to try to help this chick, I'll support you. You always support me when I have crazy ideas, so what the heck. What kind of friend would I be if I couldn't return the favor?"

"A superficial one,"

"Okay, okay already, point taken," I said, trying to get this over with.

I followed Gina's lead as she eased her way toward the young woman. She couldn't have been older than twenty years old. Gina took her time, checked out the situation, and then approached her. The music was so loud; I couldn't hear what she originally said to her, but the sister hesitantly went with us into the restroom.

"Hi, I'm Gina and this is my girlfriend, Reina. We were wondering if we could speak to you for a minute," Gina asked, diplomatically.

"Was sup," the female responded, flipping her braids from one side to the other, with her long overly designed acrylic nails?

"Oh, well . . . I noticed you out there on the dance floor dancing, and . . . well, I didn't know if you were aware that your skirt was hiked up, to your stomach," Gina said, stumbling over her words, not knowing how the girl would react.

"Ya'll call me in here for this bullshit? Of course I knew, shoot, I pulled it up there," she said, smacking on her chewing gum and pursing her lips, very irritated.

The conversation was not going the way we had planned. This female obviously felt vexed by our intrusion.

"Well, if you don't mind me asking, why would you do that?" Gina asked her, appalled at what she had just heard.

"Ya'll don't know nothin, huh? That's how you get dem busta's to buy yo drinks, all night. I don't pay for nothin. I make dem boys spend all dey funds on me. All I gotta do is roll on em a lil bit and I get anything I want up in this joint. I be making nem sucka's spend dey cash on ya girl. I be getting drinks all night and when I get hungry I make em get me a chicken plate, so was sup, ya'll need some pointers or something cause I could teach ya how da game go?" The girl said, waving her pointer finger back and forth in the air.

"Well, I guess she told us, huh Gee?"

"What's your name, friend?" Gina asked her.

"Nicole, but my peeps call me lil Nikki for short. So if ya'll done harrassin me, I need to be rockin my mouf piece for my next drink," Nikki said, bluntly.

"How about if I buy you a drink Nikki," Gina asked.

"Wha? I don't get down like dat! I'm strictly dickly, ya heard me?" Nikki blurted out.

I put my hand over my mouth to remain composed, while laughing on the inside. She thought Gina was hitting on her. That tickled my funny bone, but I couldn't laugh out loud. It would discredit what Gina was trying to achieve.

"No, I just thought that if I bought you a drink that would be one less drink you would have to hustle. That's all."

"Oh... a-ight. I thought you was tryna push up on me, lil Nikki don't roll like dat," she said, in her ebonic language.

"Alrighty then, it's settled. Let's go get that drink," Gina nudged us.

We all walked out to the bar one behind the other. Gina ordered drinks for us. I had a Bloody Mary, Gina had a Tom Collins, and Nikki had a Remy Martin. All of our drinks had names, after people. I didn't know who any of them were, but they sure tasted good. Nikki's drink must have been especially good, based on the way she stuck her gum to the back of her hand and gulped it down while holding the glass with her pinky finger sticking out.

"What are you planning to do now, buy her drinks all night, Gee?" I asked.

"If it keeps her away from those menacing looking guys, I will."

"Well that's admirable and all, but what exactly are you trying to accomplish? You might save her from getting into some trouble tonight, but what about tomorrow night and the night after?"

"I don't have all the answers, Reina. I just see an opportunity to help someone, that's all, no more, no less. She could have a promising future ahead of her, but she needs to feel good about herself first."

"I hear you girl."

"Anyway, how do you think I stay so blessed? I help people. That's what God wants us to do, right, help people? It always comes back to you. I don't know about you but I invest in my karma girl. Somebody will come and unexpectedly offer to do something for me, or give me something that they didn't even know I needed. You ought to try it sometime. It works. Believe me when I say, you reap what you sow,"

Dejavu...Wow...Lance preaches that same sermon to me time and time again. Gina was so right. When did she become all Christian-like anyway? That's why she's my best friend. She knows what to say to encourage me to be a better person. I may not like the lectures all the time, especially when they cut into my partying, but after it's all said and done, she always seems to have inspired me in some way. That was very important to me in a relationship, with anyone, to be able to grow from them, and vice versa.

The fellas approached us on our bar stools like cockroaches, asking if we wanted to dance, or buy us a drink...etc . . . ; I guess it was true in most instances; birds of a feather do flock together, because I felt like a hoochie mama, the way they were acting toward us. If they only knew, it takes a lot more than a dance and a drink to get some of this, but unfortunately, it doesn't for a lot of other undiscerning women who settle for that type of treatment. They don't respect themselves or appreciate their bodies. I have been guilty of the same thing and sometimes it's a struggle not to give in, but in the end, it has been worth every single night that I spent alone. I still have my dignity, my self-respect and most of all, my self worth. Besides that, it was a whole other world out there these days. People are dying due to a lonely night.

"Thanks for the drink; I gotta go get my dance on." Nikki said, walking away swaying and snapping her fingers to the beat of Dr. Dre's rap tune that was playing.

"Okay Nikki, it was nice to meet you," we said, in unison.

"Ya'll be cool," Nikki responded, as she blew a large smoke ring above her head from the black n mild cigar she was smoking.

Nikki grabbed the hand of a thug, with a pair of snatch-out gold teeth in his mouth that had letters and symbols inscribed in them. I caught a glimpse of him when he came over to escort her off her cushioned bar stool to the dance floor. She liked that type, the more thuggish the better. He wore all gold teeth and a white T-shirt, with a picture on it that paid homage to one of his deceased homies. His pants hung off his butt to expose his boxers, and his medallions were heavier than his own body weight. He displayed a list of several different females' names on both his arms. He looked intimidating. Personally, I would be frightened if a person like that came up to me on the street, even if his request for the time was legitimate. Getting a position in Corporate America was not on his top list of priorities and Nikki didn't care one bit. She liked the rappers and ball player types; anybody with a little bit of assets, and a ghetto swag was fine with her.

Nikki was back to her old tricks, just that fast. At some point during the night, Rowdy Red and Gangsta Slim referred to the lil Shorty that kept stealing the show and offered her a spot on stage. Nikki walked up to the sweat-ridden stage, like she owned it and spontaneously choreographed a dance routine as if it were really part of the show. Her moves were ghetto fabulously inspired, yet creative and entertaining. The crowd readily cheered her on to no end.

"Look at her, she's really good and she actually has great stage presence," said Gina.

"Yeah, I see," I said, as I supported her by bobbing my head.

"She's so confident."

"She should be a dancer in the videos," I complemented.

"It's such a shame for her to waste her talents out here like this. All she needs is the proper training,"

"Yeah, she could definitely use some etiquette training but her dance moves are fierce," I said.

"I meant dance training, girl," Gina said, laughing at me.

"Oh," I chuckled with Gina.

"Are you about ready to blow this joint or what, Gee?"

"Well, now I'm not so sure. I've taken an interest in Nikki,"

"Okay then. Hey, I'm on vacation, I can stay out all night,"

"What time is it?" She asked, looking down at my watch.

"It's one-thirty," I told her, twirling myself in a circle as if I was having the time of my life.

I guess we should get going so that we can get up early. "You still want to go by Leona's in the morning, right?" Gina asked.

"Yeah, definitely,"

Gina and I retired from the club while being pestered all the way to the exit door. The guys didn't bother us too much until they thought that we were leaving. They offered us a few drinks here and there, but I know Gina had on her do not approach me look, and I decided earlier in the day that I would try to make it work with my husband. Therefore, we must have appeared to be off limits. I am not complaining though, bearing in mind, the types of guys that were in the club. I was fine not being approached much. I don't think I'm a snob or anything, but thugs just are not my type.

On our way back to the train, I was too tired to talk. I was thinking about my Uncle Seth. He would have eaten Nikki alive if he were with us. He used to say how he needed his woman to help conduct his business by running his errands, because he was always on house arrest. He did a dime in the early seventies. He has tried to stay out of trouble, but trouble just seemed to find him. He smoked weed all day long and that was probably why he couldn't ever remember anything.

He would lie about something, and then forget the lie in a matter of seconds. I mean, in the same sentence. Having a conversation with Uncle Seth was very tiresome. He would have loved Nikki though. She was his type, lock, stock, and barrel. He wouldn't even care that she didn't speak proper English, as long as she had his back, or held his weed when the police pulled them over; he would be one hundred percent completely satisfied. She was what he called a ride or die chick. Seth told my adopted parents the reason he divorced his ex-wife Linda, was because she was a goody two shoes. He said she had exceptional morals, but that clashed with what he needed out of the relationship. My mother was mortified, but at least he was honest with himself about who he was. My mother disowned him from the family, so when I wanted to see him, I had to sneak. She forbade me to contact him, for any reason. Seth and I were close for a short time, but I always knew that he would be there for me if I ever needed him for anything.

When he first came home from prison, he spent a lot of time at our house, in Mississippi. Since Seth was my mother's baby brother, she felt a sense of obligation to help Big Mama take care of him, to relieve her of some of the responsibility. Seth would sit and tell me all kinds of unsuitable stories for a young girl, but it made us closer. I did not know Uncle Seth very well when he first went to the penitentiary. Uncle Seth was a rough neck back in the day. He hung with cold-hearted killers who are still doing time in Angola on murder charges. Word on the street was, he whacked a few rivals himself. He never admitted to any graphic details like that, but he shared a few stories with me about things that happened on the inside, or as he called it, behind the bricks.

He said that there were several cliques. The clique he was a part of consisted of just him and his fall partners, a total of five. These were the same guys he hung out with in high school. Mother did not like them. She said they were bad news. Sure enough, she was right. Uncle Seth took the dive for being in their company during one of their dope dealing heists. He was not actually involved with that particular get rich quick scheme, but there were others. He would never get too specific with me about the things him and his crew had done. He said that was to protect me. He said, if I didn't know any-thing, then I couldn't tell anything. He did the least amount of time out of all of the other boys. He did not have any paraphernalia on him, but he was in the wrong place at the wrong time.

Peewee, Skip, Peanut and Frog all got life without parole. Uncle Seth went down to the prison a couple times a year, to keep them abreast on the outside world. He and I have been at Wal-Mart and other places together; he would use those little disposable cameras to take pictures of female's backsides to send to his partners in crime. He never forgot about them. Uncle Seth had been out more than twenty years and he still tried to keep up with his homeboys. My mother couldn't appreciate the devotion my Uncle showed to his partners, because she said he wouldn't even be in this mess if it were not for those hoodlums. Uncle Seth said that he and his boys had taken turns saving each other's lives time after time and no one needed to understand it, other than the participating parties. Even though the acts were criminal, the way they watched each other's back and looked out for one another was . . . unfathomable. To show that kind of loyalty and commitment to another human being was admirable in some remotely complex sense.

Uncle Seth received letters from each of them once every couple of months. I can't imagine their lives being that exciting where they needed to write so many letters. I guess they were just bored. There was probably only so much basketball and weight lifting they could do. Writing was their outlet, the way they stayed connected to the outside world.

Mother did not like Uncle Seth getting mail from those guys at our house. She didn't want them to know where we lived. She said that she was scared for her life. Unc didn't have anywhere else to have them send the mail, so he defied her rules and had the mail sent there anyway. That was why about a decade and a half ago mom and pops packed up our immediate family and moved us to Memphis where shortly after Pop started his own church.

Big Mama did not mind Seth getting mail or anything else at her house. She always said that the good Lord would take care of her, rest her soul. Not to mention, she loved the ground her son walked on. Even though Seth was the black sheep of the family, he was by far Big Mama's favorite. Everybody knew it. Mother was jealous growing up, but she learned that was never going to change, so it was best she just accept it. Big Mama loved all seven of her children dearly, but she and Seth shared a special bond that no one could ever break, not even my mother, and she has tried on several occasions.

Rumor had it that Big Mama had outside relations with the true love of her life, Deacon Henry Mack whom she had known since they were young. They attended church together. He was the Deacon at the small Southern Baptist church they attended as children. Big Mama could never get Big Daddy to go to church with her. She and Big Daddy had a good relationship over all, but only one thing was missing. Big Daddy wasn't saved much less sanctified, or filled with the Holy Ghost. He would chew tobacco and drink wine every day. He was a hard worker, though. He would bring his check home and put it right in Big Mama's hands. Big Mama obviously was in love with Deacon Mack her whole life, but she was faithful to Big daddy, until one-day, she lost her religion, right there in the Pastor's office of the church. It was right after the Deacon Mack delivered the sermon. The pastor let Deacon Mack deliver the sermon sometimes because he was getting ready to ordain him to be a full fledge minister. Big Mama was in awe that day. I believe she saw in him what she had wished she had in her own husband, a Christian man, with potential to have his own congregation one day. She couldn't contain it any longer. After the members had all gone for the evening she fell into his arms and they sinned together. Big Mama always felt so guilt-stricken about sinning in the Lords house that she never forgave herself. Shortly after Seth was born, her health quickly started to decline. Big Mama blamed it on her abominable sin. Some say that was why she also had such a strong connection to Seth. His conception was out of pure passion. Everyone was elated about the new baby coming. There was a ten-year gap between Seth and his older brother, Adam. Big Daddy was also thrilled. He could hardly wait for Seth's arrival. He hand-crafted and stained a wooden baby crib with his bare hands. Big Daddy was very handy.

As the story was told to me, Seth was born and Deacon Mack would come over to the house to visit him. He took on the role of Godfather. He would bring money and gifts. He and Big Daddy would go in the backroom and privately talk for hours and hours. Nobody knew why.

Deacon Mack would visit Seth in the prison as his Godfather, un-til he found out that he was terminally ill. Deacon Mack had devel-oped colon cancer and felt compelled to reveal the truth to Seth. He said he had lived all those many years as his Godfather and his last dying wish was to live the last few months as his real father, which blew Seth away. He could not explain the liking that he had had for the Deacon for all of those years. He called me one day unexpectedly and told me the whole story. I was blown away to find out such a shocking family secret. He said that Big Daddy knew all about it the whole time, but refused to leave his wife whom he had loved all of his life. Big Daddy made a decision to keep things quiet forever and love Seth as his own, and he did. Shortly after that visit from the Deacon, he passed away and Seth became withdrawn from having interper-sonal dealings with others. He didn't know who he was anymore. He started compulsively telling lies for no reason at all. He wondered why he was so different from all of his other siblings. He had such a rebellious spirit and a different personality than the rest of the family. Everyone had their own way about them, but Seth was the most different, even right down to his cynical sense of humor. All of the other siblings lived upright and Christian lives. Seth loved a chal-lenge. He took pride in knowing how much dirt he could get away with.

He now has his own place in Connecticut, thanks to the inher-itance money that Mack left him. It was enough to set him on his feet when he got out of prison. He moved as far away from the family as possible. He felt betrayed by Big Daddy who knew who his real father was all of that time and did not tell him. He would have wanted to spend more time with the Deacon, getting to know his side of the family. He was Mack's only heir and when he died, he left Seth his whole life's savings. Seth inherited his house in Woodville and eighteen thousand dollars that he saved just for him. Seth rented the house out in the country to a family of five that also attended the church where we all grew up, that was Seth's way of trying to keep Mack's memory alive, by associating with people that knew him well. He went there several times a year to get together with them to talk about Mack and how dedicated he was to the church. Sometimes the tenants couldn't pay all of the rent and Seth let them slide, because they were such good friends of his father. Seth has definitely had a hard life. I call him sometimes just to say hi, against Mother's will. I thought about calling him while I was in New York since he only lived a hop, skip, and a jump away. We had a lot of catching up to do. I wanted to tell him all about Lance and me. They had never met, only spoken on the phone a couple of times. Then after thinking about it, I decided not to tell him about Lance and me. I didn't want to stir up any feelings of hostility in Seth, because I knew what he was capable of, so I left well enough alone.

When arriving at our stop I noticed that Gina looked a little down. She hardly said two words to me on the ride home. I just figured that she was exhausted as I was, so there was very little interaction on the short walk home. I needed to call Lance, but I thought that I would wait until the morning. I was sure he was getting his beauty rest.

# Chapter 7

"Hi Mama Lee," I said, when she met us at the door holding a beer, staggering and talking loudly. Mama Lee hugged me even tighter than Gina did when she first saw me.

"Girl, where on earth have you been? I sure have missed you," she said with a lit cigarette dangling out of the left side of her mouth.

"Mama, why are you yelling? We can hear you."

"Girl, you know that's just how I talk. Anyway where have you been? You was supposed to come over here a week ago to help me write my living will and testament."

"I know mama, but I'm here now, aren't you glad to see me?" Gina asked, playfully pouting.

"I suppose, you little knuckle head girl," she said, sipping on her canned cocktail.

"Why are you writing a will Mama Lee, It's not like you're going anywhere anytime soon?" I asked, to lighten the mood a little.

"Girl please; the way I drink this devil's juice and puff on these cancer sticks. I never know when it'll be time to go meet my maker. I just want to be prepared so that my baby girl here inherits this big empire of mine, but ya'll can't have my darling Jimmy because I will come back and haunt the both of you."

"Mama, will you please stop talking crazy. You'll put a damper on the visit."

"Oh, that girl ain't thinkin bout what I'm sayin. You are gettin to be too sensitive in your old age, Gina. Chill out, shit!" Mama said, holding up her middle and index finger to gesture the peace sign.

"Oh Lord Mama, you are getting more ghetto by the minute," Gina expressed.

"Let's all sit down and get comfortable," said Mama, as she plopped into her recliner.

"So, where's Mister Jimmy?" Gina asked.

"Oh, my snuckums is in there, with his ole funky behind. I keep tellin that man to stop layin all over my nice clean sheets without takin a shower first. He gets off work, and then comes straight over here, smellin like the food he don cooked at work."

"Can I see him Mama Lee? I'm just so excited for you. Let me take a peek at him," I said.

"Girl no, you might see his bigum?" Mama Lee asked.

"His bigum?" I asked, confused.

"Well, if you peek yo head through that door, you gon see a bigum." Mama Lee said, laughing.

"Mama, please don't start with the dirty jokes. You're embarrassing me."

I had to laugh myself. Mama Lee was so much fun to be around, even though she drove Gina crazy with all of her ghetto fabulous gestures and antics.

"Hmmmmmm," my cell phone vibrated.

"Hello," I answered. "Oh, hey sweetie, I miss you . . . Huh? ... What do you mean? ...I didn't feel the phone vibrating through my purse, the music was really loud . . . The club . . . Uh, club Jigga . . . Me and Gina . . ."

"Uh oh," Gina mumbled.

"Just me and Gina, why... But why Lance, Look I'm by Mama Leona's house right now, I'll have to call you back . . . I will . . . I said I will, calm down . . ."

"You better tell that lil nappy head boy I said to take it down a notch. He don't be calling my house startin no stuff nah," Mama Lee said, struggling to get up from her chair. She even put her beer down for this one. Mama Lee loved a good fight. She was always fussing and fighting with her neighbors, over issues like their dogs pooping on the sidewalk in front of her building.

"Mama, what did I tell you about getting involved in other people's business?" said Gina.

Mama Lee could hardly pull her scrawny body up from the sunken in cushions of the recliner, but she talked smack all the way up. She had my back. When she finally did get up, she stood over me rocking back and forth and reaching for the phone. I was waiting to see which direction the falling ash from her cigarette would fly as she waved her arms around in circles.

"Gimme that phone! You ain't on trial," said Mama Lee, reaching in further.

"I have to go now Lance. Gotta go . . . Call you later, bye," I said, rushing him off the phone before Leola got a hold of it. That would've been a real mess.

"Why didn't you let me say a thing or two to him? What's wrong with him? He gon give himself a heart attack worryin bout what you doin. Ya'll young people today is somethin else. Ya'll need to learn how to rest your lil nerves."

We heard the bedroom door open and out walked this tall dark chocolate man.

"Well Lee, you didn't tell me we had company, dear," said Jimmy, rubbing his eyes.

"How could I, you was snorin . . . I mean restin so good. I didn't want to wake you honey," said Mama Lee in a peaceful tone. Mama Lee had gone from wanting to kick Lance's butt over the phone to being as sweet as pie.

"Well, hello Gina, who's your friend here?" asked Jimmy.

"This is my friend Reina, from New Orleans. She's the one I always speak of."

"Yes, of course. How do you do Reina?" Jimmy asked, kissing the back of my hand.

Wow, what a charming man Mama Lee has landed for herself. I was impressed.

"Hold up there, Jimmy, you know I don't allow you to be smoochin down no other ladies nah," scolded Mama Lee, playfully.

I hope she wasn't serious. I would hate to find myself caught in one of Mama Lee's drunken brawls, especially when it would feature... me.

"Would you like me to come over there and smooch you, my pumpkin pie?" Jimmy asked her.

"Why yes I would, as a matter of fact."

"Now you know that's never a problem with me, honey cakes," he said walking sexily over to her, reaching his arms out lovingly.

"That does it," said Gina, "We're out of here. You guys are disgusting. Yuck! Like I want to see my momma make out. Reina get your purse," demanded Gina.

"Alright Leona, you be good you hear?" I said, laughing at her.

"Never," she responded.

"I love you, Leona, and it was really nice meeting you Jimmy," I told her.

"Same here Ms. Reina. Have a safe trip back home. Hope to see you again," said Jimmy.

We all hugged, kissed, and said our goodbyes. I hated to leave. I was having a grand time watching the two of them fondle one another. Especially at their age, to see them all in love was a treat.

"Girl, did you see how they acted in there? That's just gross."

"No, it's not Gee. Don't you think you're overreacting just a little?"

"No, I don't."

"She's happy Gee. Don't take that away from her!"

"I know, I know. I truly want her to be happy, but it almost seems . . . unnatural or something."

"Unnatural, how so?"

"Okay look. What would a stud like Jimmy want with a woman about to turn sixty, when he can obviously have a pretty, young thing, ya know?

"How are we supposed to know why people do the strange things they do? We aren't psychologists."

"That's right. So since we don't know what his true motives are, what's wrong with keeping an eye on him?"

"Nothing, I guess. But, how do you know that Leona doesn't have motives of her own?"

"I don't."

"Well, Hallelujah. I think we just had a breakthrough."

"Forget you Gina," we laughed.

"Girl, your mom is a smart woman. She can handle herself, trust me."

"I hope you're right Reina. I sure hope you're right."

Gina and I headed back to the brownstone to shower and change our clothes. We were going out again. Lance did not like the fact that I had been out all night and I was sure he did not like it that night either, but I was on vacation. I was going out! He was just going to have to get over it. Just like I had to when he did something I did not like.

"What's the plan for tonight Gina?"

"I thought we'd go down to this spot in Manhattan. Can you dig it, baby?" said Gina, doing her hippy impression.

"I can dig it," I responded, rubbing my hands together in excitement.

"I know you can, girl. I know you can," said Gina.

Gina and I headed back to her house to spend a little quality time together before our next excursion on the subway.

Finally, it was time to relax on Gina's olive colored reclining leather sectional. She went in the kitchen, whipped us up some snacks, nachos with cheese, ice cream, and last but not least, a slice of strawberry cheesecake. We talked awhile, laughed and got all caught up, when something on television caught my eye. A newsbreak interrupted the program we were watching. They were showing a picture of the outside of club Jigga. I tried to read the newscasters lips as he spoke, while we fumbled around looking for the Universal remote control that I found buried behind all of the pillows that decorated the sofa.

The newscaster proceeded to talk about a young black female whose name they couldn't release as of yet, until they were able to notify the family. They said she had been gang raped and brutally bludgeoned to death. Waste Management found her bloody, naked body in the long metal dumpster that extended parallel to the club in the alley when they came to pick up the trash. The story went on to say that, the young woman had been disfigured so badly from all of the hard blows to the face and body that they may have to identify her from a canine ex-ray, just to be sure of who she was. There were no suspects or evidence as of yet, until an autopsy was performed. The culprits stripped her completely of her clothes. There was one black high heel boot recovered from the crime scene. They dusted the scene for fingerprints.

Gina and I could not believe what we had just seen and heard. I turned to look at her and she had a couple of tears streaming down her face with her mouth wide open. We just sat in silence feeling numb from the shock. We knew exactly who the young woman was that they referred to as Jane Doe.

"Oh, my God," Gina exclaimed.

I concurred with her sentiment. We sat quietly and watched the police officers pace back and forth through the yellow tape.

"Look Gee! Wasn't that the guy who we talked to at the club?"

"Which guy?"

"The guy who drank water all night,"

"Sure was girl. That's him alright. You were right on about him. Sorry for doubting you."

"Yeah, I knew he was a cop. I just knew it!"

"They said they found a high heel boot. Nikki was wearing high heel boots."

"Reina, my gut tells me it's her. I hope to God it's not, but I just have a bad feeling."

"I know me too."

As we returned to our regularly scheduled program, Gina turned to me for comfort. I did not know what to say. I needed comforting myself. We were just with this chick last night. How could she be dead today? It did not seem real. She was so happy and full of life last night.

"Reina, I think subconsciously I knew something bad was going to happen. That's why I tried so hard to reach out to her but she just would not listen to save her life, literally," said Gina.

"Are you serious Gee? Are you psychic or something?"

"On some small level, I think so. Sometimes I can sense things before they actually happen."

"Really, I had no idea? Has it always been that way?"

"Well I've always been intuitive, but it really started to develop when I became a Christian."

"Well, how does it work?" I asked, curiously.

"It's not like I can say for sure that something will or won't happen but sometimes things involuntarily come to my mind and I don't know why. Like Nikki for instance, why did I feel so drawn to her? Maybe I was supposed to do something."

"Like what Gee? What else could you have done for her? She was rude to us and obviously did not want to be bothered."

"Yeah, I know it appeared that way, but I should've tried a different tactic to grab her attention."

"I think you are putting too much responsibility on yourself. You don't even know her."

"Reina, do you remember how you and I first met?"

"Sure, we met in high school."

"Yes, but what was the circumstance?"

"Oh, you mean when you saved my butt from getting kicked in the girl's bathroom?"

"Uh yeah, that would be the time. Actually, my classes were on the other side of the school, so it was highly unlikely for me to go into the bathroom where you were. That day, I got my hall pass during third period and went to my usual restroom on the third floor. Someone had just been in there, obviously, because it reeked of their gastric track backing up, like a sewer. That's how I ended up in the bathroom on the second floor where you were. I had to go bad, too. I don't know why, but I remember it like it was yesterday. In I walked and there you were, on the floor, swinging your arms like you were shooing flies."

"Okay, okay. You don't have to rub it in, girl."

"Alright I won't rub it in. I just sense things. Like when people are in trouble."

"I can't lie. You saved my butt that time, girl. I owe you one. That chick was huge too."

"Reina, girl you owe me so many, I've lost count."

"More breaking news, Gina look!"

The announcer ripped our hearts out when he said that the girls name was Nicole Rochelle Wilson.

"Oh no Gina, it's her for sure. Oh my God, Oh my God,"

"Yep, poor little Nikki,"

"How are we supposed to go out tonight after this, my trip was ruined?"

"I know what you mean, but don't say your trip is ruined! You are alive and well aren't you?"

"Well . . . yes."

"Then it's not ruined. We are still going to enjoy your visit. It's nothing we can do for her now."

"I just feel so awful."

"You're human, so that's a normal feeling. I feel bad too, but we can't let it destroy your trip, no matter what."

"Yeah, I know you're right," I said.

"So, do you still want to go out, or would you rather stay in?"

"Let's stay in tonight. My flight leaves in the morning at ten-thirty anyway. This can be just as much fun. What movies do you have on the mantle?"

"Let's see here."

"I'm in the mood for a comedy."

"I understand. I really do. We need to lighten this mood."

"How about something old, like *Waiting to Exhale* or something like that?"

"Reina do you know how many times I've seen that movie, too many?"

"Okay then. It really doesn't matter. Put anything in there and let's get some popcorn started."

"How did you know I have popcorn, you been raiding my cabinets?"

"Of course I have Gee. You should've known that."

Gina decided on *Big Momma's House*, while I popped the popcorn. We soon went to sleep right there on the couch. Morning came so quickly. I got up, dressed, had breakfast, packed my last bit of toiletry, hugged Gina, and headed back home.

I could not wait to get home and give Lance the best lovin he ever had. I missed him. I honestly missed him especially after what happened to Nikki. I felt like I needed a hug and Lance's hugs were the best. They are warm and passionate.

Seeing Gina again was so nice. It brought back a lot of memories; some I want to remember and some I want to forget. Gina and I were terrible back in our day. Maybe one day I will write a book about it. Then I was on my way to see my husband and make things good between us, Really Good, if you know what I mean.

# Chapter 8

As I walked from the Delta terminal, to the baggage claim area, there he stood, holding Rose in my satchel and watching the people drag their two and three-piece luggage sets from the conveyer belt. I was so excited to see Lance. He looked incredible, standing there in his dark denim jeans, Sean John button down shirt and khaki Timberland boots. I glided toward him in slow motion, watching every move he made, to my delight. I passed a pole and I couldn't resist taking a leisurely moment to stare at him in admiration. He was by far the finest man I had ever been with. I didn't want to blink my eyes. Every move and gesture he made sparkled with class. As I watched, I undressed him with my eyes. Although I knew very well what was underneath his clothes, I allowed my imagination to run wild by fantasizing about his chiseled naked body. This man was so fine, watching him struck the retina of my eye in such a way, it caused my blood pressure to raise and my pulse to quicken. He was completely oblivious to me lurking from behind the pole, but it induced a psychosomatic thrill for me. I almost felt like a stalker. The longer I watched him, the more stimulated I became. I began walking over to him. He caught a glance of me from ten feet away and greeted his wife very properly, with wide opened arms, a big dimpled smile, a tight warm hug, a gentle passionate kiss and a soft-spoken "Hey babe." That was all he said and was all he needed to say. The rest was understood. One of the many things that I loved was that we didn't have to say too much to each other and it felt just as good, as if we had said a mouth full.

Lance retrieved my Louis Vuitton luggage for me, and then we walked out to the parking lot. I couldn't deny the stars that occupied my eyes when I looked at him. I was in love with my husband once again. Thank God.

"You hungry babe," Lance asked, as he carefully backed out of the two white lines that our car sat between?

"Hungry for you," I responded, looking deep into his eyes.

"Really, well say no more," he said, while pressing his index finger gently against my lips as we drove down the ramp, into the sunset.

Lance knew how to make my body shiver by barely touching me; sometimes without touching me at all. I love a man that knows how to arouse my emotional g-spot. That is an exceptionally discerning triumph in a relationship, when a man takes his time to get to know his woman to the point where he can practically take her into an orgasmic state, just by looking into her eyes, talking to her soul with his. Any man that has mastered that fine art should feel free to pat himself on the back. Unfortunately, some men think that if they can make a woman sore, raw and walk funny the next day, due to him beating it up all night while she screamed and hollered and then she fell fast asleep afterwards, he has done his job and that was all that was necessary. Not for a woman like me; I need substance. I want a well-rounded man. One who satisfies me in every way, emotionally, intellectually, physically, financially, everything! That was my Lance. He was definitely on his job.

When we arrived at the door of our condominium Lance wanted to carry me inside, as he did the day we got married.

"Babe, do you remember our wedding day when I carried you over the threshold?"

"Of course I do. How could I ever forget the best day of my life?"

"Well, I want to reenact that day. You may have gained a pound or two but I think I can make it."

"Boy, you better watch it. You know you love all of this."

"I can't deny it. You're right babe. I love it with all my heart."

Lance picked me up and carried me straight to the bedroom. He had prepared a romantic evening. He had our favorite compilation disk playing, rose petals that adorned the entire room and he lit a couple of scented candles to top it all off. The trouble that he had gone to was priceless. Little did he know, he had me at hello! I was not going to tell him that right away though. I wanted to enjoy every little detail of what Lance had in store for me. He laid me back on the bed and began slowly taking off my shoes.

"Baby, why don't you let me run and take a quick shower? I've been traveling and . . ."

"No, I want you just as you are," he said guiding my right hand where he wanted it.

"But baby, I would feel more comfortable if I could just . . ."

"I want to inhale your femininity Reina. Don't worry, I love the way you smell," he said softly, nibbling my left earlobe.

"Well, alright. It's not like I'm dirty or anything. I just want to be perfectly fresh for you."

"You are incredibly beautiful to me right now," Lance said, as he licked his tongue all the way up my left leg.

I love when he licks me. Lance was a professional when it came to matters of the bedroom. Next, he worked his way back down to my toes and slowly sucked them one by one. There wasn't much more that he could do to me at this point. I was almost where I wanted to be. I must give credit where credit is due. Lance definitely knew his woman, inside and out, literally. He took his sweet time making his way up to the candy shop. He finally got there and I heard what sounded like a sniff. I could not believe it. I knew something was funny when he denied me a shower. He wanted to see if I smelled like sex. That dirty dog! I was pissed. Believe that!

It never failed, as quickly as that man could put me in the mood, he could take me right out. I just couldn't believe how much he distrusted me. Well, then again, yes I can; damn, right when I was about to get mine too. I should have known something was up though. He was being excessively sweet.

"Whoa, Lance, did you just sniff me?" I asked, in a perplexed tone, frowning at him through my legs.

"Babe, stop trippin. It's not a big deal. I was just making sure my stuff was still mine and untouched, that's all."

"That's all? And why wouldn't it be untouched?"

"Reina, you know how you are when you get a few drinks in you. You get flirtatious."

"Says who, you?"

"Says whoever's looking."

"Okay Lance. Look, I admit, when a person drinks they become altered to a degree, depending on how much they drank, but by no means does that make me a hoe. I can control myself in public. I know how to resist temptations and I don't succumb to peer pressure. Not to mention the fact that I am in a committed relationship, with you."

I rolled out of the bed and put my jeans back on.

"Reina, you are overreacting, as usual. Nobody called you a hoe."

"You may as well have. You don't trust me to believe I was faithful."

"Well . . . were you faithful?"

"You know what Lance, I'm gonna be honest with you. When I left you last Friday, I had my mind set on meeting somebody, anybody for that matter, not because I was drinking either. I made that decision sober, even before I left New Orleans. I was sick to death of you, your mama, and your whole doggone family. I was hoping to meet somebody interesting that I could get to know. But you know what Lance? After talking to Gina, the very person who you don't want me to be around, because of your own insecurities, I decided against it. I had every good intention of coming home to you and trying to make it work between us, but you found a way to screw that up. That's wassup, if you really wanna know."

"You better watch what you say to me. Once you say it, you can't take it back Reina."

"Whatever! I know exactly what the hell I'm saying and I don't wanna take it back."

"Reina, why are you talking all... ghetto, you're not a man? You need to stay in a woman's place."

"I know I'm not a man! Maybe you think I have turned into a man, because you sure don't act like you got a woman at home waiting on you day in and day out. Why don't we check and see if I'm a man or not?"

Lance made me so mad and I was completely out of character. I lost all of the ingredients of being a sophisticated lady that I had acquired over the years, just that fast and involuntarily exposed the unladylike side of my personality, which I had tried so hard to suppress. In other words, Sheniq-wa, my alter ego was here in full effect.

I came out of my jeans that I just put back on less than thirty seconds ago and showed Lance that I was not a man.

"Since you wanna sniff it so bad, come put your whole face in it and get a good whiff! Come on! What, you scared?" I condescendingly said, pulling my labia apart.

"Oh my God, who are you right now? Don't start something you can't finish!" Lance said, pointing at me and shifting his weight from one foot to the other.

"Oh you best believe I can finish it. Come on wit it! What are you waiting for, the bus? Come over here and put your face deep in it and I hope you suffocate yourself, you insecure jerk."

I used my thumbs and index fingers to spread myself as wide as an eagle spreads its wings at full flight and beckoned Lance to come investigate my gender, to ensure that we never had to have this conversation again.

"You have really lost it this time Reina. I always knew you were crazy but to act like this puts you over the top," Lance said, shaking his head in disbelief.

"Lance I could care less what you think of me right now, so you can keep your little smart-ass comments to yourself."

"I know you don't care and that's the problem."

"No, you're the problem, ole insecure punk."

"I've already told you to watch your mouth!"

"Are you gonna come over here and sniff or not, so I can close my lips and get on with my damn day?"

"I don't have time for your stupid games. I'm going to my mama's."

"Good! Maybe she'll let you sniff her, since you're over there all the time, you stinkin mamas' boy."

"What did you say?"

The altitude in his voice heightened, as he slowly walked toward me with his head cocked to the side.

"I asked you a question Reina. Mind repeating what you said?"

He took one big step close to me, put his right hand tightly around my neck, and slowly escorted me backwards to the wall, as if he was going to choke me, if I said another word. I think I hallucinated for a split second because I swear I saw fangs. I am not crazy. I can read body language very well and it was probably not in my best interest to repeat myself. I stood there in amazement. Lance had never put his hands on me before. I must have really pushed a button this time. Yeah, talking about a man's mama is not such a smart idea. Lance had a look in his eyes that I did not ever recall seeing before. It was even more intense than the one he gave Johnny at the party. It was scary.

I read in the newspaper some time back about how a man strangled his wife with his bare hands for mouthing off to him. You just never know what will make a person click. Nothing was worth losing my life over, though. Not even having the last word and I love having the last word, but I'm glad I let that one go. Lance let go of my neck, grabbed his keys, and walked out. He slammed the door so hard behind him that the whole condominium shook like one of California's earthquakes at 7.0 on the Richter scale.

I waited motionless until I was sure he was not coming back inside. I peeked around the corner of the bedroom and down the stairs and said "yeah, go suck on your mama's saggin titties, you punk-ass mama's boy". I just had to have the last word. It made me feel better, even if he didn't hear what I said. I said it and that was all that mattered to me.

I was tired from the flight, so I lay down on the bed face up, allowing my head to sink deep into the fluffy pillow. I figured Lance would be gone all day. That was a relief in itself that I didn't have to lay eyes on him for a while.

I had taken a Tylenol PM for the headache that I developed. Before I knew it, I had slept through the entire night. I crept downstairs; found Lance asleep in our library, on the couch. I tiptoed down the hall, past the wall sconces back to the bedroom in an attempt not to wake him. I lay back down because I knew at seven o'clock he would be leaving for work. I just calmly rested, awaiting his departure. I pulled the covers as far up to my head as they could go and rested, thinking about what had transpired between us a few hours ago. I got up and saw that he was finally gone. I followed through with my morning routine as if I were going to work, but I took the day off because I needed to recuperate from my trip.

I sat on my side of the bed and made out a to-do list, like I did every morning, so I wouldn't forget to run all of my errands. I thanked God for all of his blessings and then started my day.

# Chapter 9

I was standing in line at Danny and Clyde's Deli, getting ready to order a mouth-watering hot sausage Po' boy dressed, when our eyes met. He looked as if he had just gotten off work when he positioned himself in line two persons behind me. It was love at first sight . . . or lust . . . or whatever. He had on a pair of old, dirty work pants; a ragged T-shirt that I think was supposed to be white and tennis shoes with a medium-sized hole in the toe. I couldn't believe I noticed all of that in the five seconds it took him to walk from the door to the line. I don't normally go for the scruffy-type, but he was different. He seemed so peaceful and calm in spirit. He had a certain strut about him that had me intrigued. He had a quiet demeanor about himself that I couldn't help noticing. I turned around in his direction a couple of times, acting as if I were looking at the people seated at the small wooden tables behind him, just so I could get a peripheral peek at him. Every time I did that, he caught me. I was trying so hard not to be obvious but my neck seemed to have a mind of its own.

I could tell that underneath all of the layers of dirt stood a mild-mannered, easy-going, gentle man who did not feel like he had to be macho at all times. What I could not see about him, I could gather from his humble aura that he would definitely take his time with a woman. He looked like he had muscles, too. This six foot, caramel-colored man with dread locks... and obviously a job, had truly captured my attention.

"Hot sausage up," the short, round stocky woman wearing a worn hair net hollered from behind the counter. I had already lost my appetite. I was on a mission to get his attention; although, I couldn't bring myself to be obvious about trying to steal his heart in a matter of minutes. I slowly grabbed my brown paper bag with a grease stain on the bottom and headed toward the door to make a hasty exit when I heard, "Excuse me sister, you dropped something." I turned to him; he was smiling, pointing his index finger at the little white receipt that must have fallen from my bag. Wow, I thought, I did it again! I found another handsome guy with a fantastic smile. The stranger had wound me up me, just that fast. I could always spot a diamond in the rough. I was subtle, sexily bending forward to pick it up when the stranger reached down to retrieve it for me. He handed it to me, still smiling a flirtatious smile. Hmm, and a gentleman too, I thought.

"Thank you," I said, smiling back at him, flinging my lightly fragrant hair as I walked out, and hoping he would follow.

I didn't want the other oblivious patrons in the store to see the unmistakable lust in my eyes, so I swaggered to my BMW, put the top down and climbed into my seat. My hair tumbled over my left eye as I pretended that I was talking on my cell phone. I didn't know how else to stall until he came out.

Oh my God, here he comes, I thought, as he walked out of the store. I didn't want this opportunity to pass me by as so many others probably had. I never gave anybody the time of day before because I was with Lance, my one and only enchanted love. The man came walking up to my car with his own grease stained brown paper bag of whatever, and a soda.

"The cashier asked me if I would bring this to you. You get a free fountain drink with your purchase of a sandwich," he said, reaching over the car door, handing me the drink.

"Oh yeah, I knew that," I chuckled.

"It's lemonade. I hope that's okay?"

"Oh, it's great. Fantastic, I love lemonade."

I could not believe, I, of all people was speechless. It was something about him that had me so outside of myself, but I couldn't put my finger on it. That guy was nothing like my type at all, mainly due to the fact that he had a blue collar job. That thing was really throwing me off. It was obvious he did construction, dug ditches or something in the manual labor industry. I guess I was just so used to Lance carrying his engraved black leather Kenneth Cole briefcase to his corner office with a view of the city every day. I wouldn't know what it was like to have a man coming home all dirty and stinking when he got off work. That for sure would be my biggest challenge. It would definitely put a damper on our sex life if I couldn't rape him as soon as he walked through the door.

I almost felt like he knew I was stalling to get a chance to talk to him. I was feeling more and more like an idiot by the second.

"You have a wonderful day, my beautiful sister," he smiled softly and walked away.

He was leaving. I thought I had better say something to make him stay a little longer. I didn't know what to say though, because I wasn't in the habit of picking up men.

"What's your name?" I asked, looking at him with a girlish innocence.

He turned back toward me and said, "Kenneth, Kenneth Baxter,"

"Well my name is Reina, in case you were wondering," I smiled.

"Very nice to meet you, Reina,"

"Do you live nearby Kenneth?"

"I do, I live a few streets away," he said, covering his mouth as he coughed.

"No kidding?"

"Seriously, I guess this place is just convenient for me, when I'm in the mood for a Po' boy,"

"Oh, so you don't know how to cook then huh?"

"What, quite the contrary, I'm an excellent cook."

"Really, what's your specialty?"

"Which one, I have so many?" He laughed.

It was so refreshing to meet a man that could cook and not have to rely on a woman and by woman, I mean me, to do it all of the time. What a relief.

"Any one of them,"

"Well, one of my favorites would have to be my beef tenders en merlot."

"Mmm, what's that?" I asked, licking my lips.

"That's when I sauté beef cubicles in red wine and demy-glace them with mushrooms. I serve that with garlic mashed potatoes and green beans almandine."

"That sounds incredible," I said, waiting for the inevitable invitation.

"Yeah, it's okay."

He was modest too. That was a turn on for me. I was so used to Lance bragging about the things he was good at.

"So what time is dinner?" I asked, eagerly.

"You want me to cook my favorite dish for you?"

"I would love to try it. Maybe I can learn a thing or two from you."

"I don't have much company over, usually."

"Really," I said, impressed.

A man who was not a playa, was this really happening to me? He cooks and he was fine being single until the right one came along, I presumed.

"No, I just chill by myself or my ex-wife drops my son off to visit with me."

"Oh, how old is he?"

"He's six."

"How cute, is his name little Kenny Jr.?"

"Absolutely,"

"So what's up for dinner? Are you up for the challenge or what?"

"It's not a challenge. It actually comes very naturally to me, since I used to be a cook when I worked off shore. I suppose it'll be okay."

"You sound apprehensive. Would you rather me not come?"

"No, it's not that."

"Then what's wrong Kenneth?"

"Never mind, how about you come over Friday night at seven?"

"Done,"

Kenny gave me his phone number to call him to confirm Friday's date. I was so excited, I could've jumped up and down right then, but he was watching. I couldn't show him my crazy side right away. I had to make him like me first.

We said our goodbyes. I took a deep breath and held it until he was all the way out of sight. Now I had to go home and face Lance. He probably wouldn't be there anyway. What did I have to worry about, except for the fact that I was already in love with the stranger from the deli.

The phone almost rang off the hook, as I hurried to unlock the door.

"Hello," I answered.

"Hey babe, I was just calling to see if you made it home alright,"

"Uh, yeah, I'm here," I said, stumbling over my words.

"Okay then. Do you need anything because I'm going over to Mike's house to help him work on his car? He needs a new transmission," He said, as if we didn't even argue last night.

Lance was tripping if he thought everything was back to normal, because it was not.

"No, I'm fine," I said, repulsed at his every word.

"Alright then babe, see you later,"

"Bye," I responded, trying to hold back the regurgitation that was developing in the back of my throat.

I hung up the phone so fast, so that I could start thinking about my new friend Kenny. First, I needed to share this news with somebody. I thought, I had better call Kayla, just to get it off my chest. I hoped she was home, so I did not have to listen to Anita Baker sing, "I apologize" in its entirety, since she threw Luther out of the house again and she's too proud to ask him back. They break up at least once a month and every time they do, she plays a song especially for him on her answering machine. He would make up a reason to call her, hear the song, think it was sweet and that's how they ended up getting back together, every time, it never failed. That's just how they do.

"Hi, you've reached Kayla's answering machine. I can't get to the phone right now, so leave a message, beep." Hmm...no song, they must've made up, I thought.

"Hey girl, where are you? I need to speak to you. You'll never believe what I picked up at the deli today. Call me!" I said, anxiously.

I went into the kitchen to prepare dinner for Lance when he arrived, "maybe chicken, and jambalaya with a demy-glazed cyanide sauce to top it off?" I asked myself, aloud. Being around Kenny for a couple of minutes had inspired me to be creative in my own cooking style. I looked in the fridge and it was almost completely bare. So were the cabinets. "Damn, that man is greedy, I thought to myself."

Every little remote thought of him started to make me twinge. He was always on my nerves, nagging me about this or that. After a while, I learned how to tune him out. He hated when I did that because he knew I was honestly not listening. I didn't care if he was mad, what about me? I was mad, too. I was mad that I had to wake up to his jealous butt every morning. However, I learned to deal with everything in my own way. My relationship with Lance had become very similar to brushing my teeth every morning. It was just something that I was supposed to do.

It was seven-thirty and no Lance. Kayla had not returned my phone call either. I was so anxious to discuss Kenny with her. I would call Gina, but I already knew what she would say. She would tell me to stop whining. I just don't feel like a lecture right now. I knew Kayla would throw her hands up and say, "Whatever makes you happy, girl."

"Hello," I answered the phone quickly, hoping it was Kayla.

"Hey boo," said Kayla, on the other end.

"Girl, you are gonna live a long time. I was just sitting here thinking about you and trying to make dinner for this fool," I said, disgustedly.

"Yeah right, since when do you cook Reina?"

"Since Lance added that to my list of chores around the house. He says that I've had a free ride long enough. He expects dinner on the table every night."

"Girl, you mean to tell me, little timid Lance has finally put his foot down?"

"Seems that way, huh?"

"You failed to tell me that lil bit of information. That's a trip. So how are you dealing with it?"

"It's okay. I just hit him up harder in the pocket, that's all."

"Who did the cooking when ya'll first met?"

"We ate out or ordered in. Now he's talking all this stuff about me pulling my weight. I think he's been talking to his co-workers, ole playa hating Negros. They just hate on him because they don't have a corner office with a view like Lance, so they try to instigate in his relationship."

"Cooking is just not your forte. What about all of the other things that you do for him, Reina, do they count for anything?"

"Yeah girl I know, huh, what about those things? I know I'm good to this man. All of his boys are jealous of him."

"Well that's because you got a big booty and they want you to go drop it like it's hot on them."

"No girl, for real. I'm always popping up to his office, bringing him lunch that I bought of course. I wear something easily accessible so I can break him off right there on his desk, and girl, I don't know if I told you but I can suck a mean . . ."

"Whoa! That's way too much information. Just stop right there."

"Anyway, you know what I'm saying girl. He sure don't complain then."

"Of course he doesn't. Why would he?"

"Well he needs to be fair and calculate the score accurately."

"You should start keeping a score sheet of your own from now on."

"No need. That's what I've been trying to tell you."

"Oh yeah, what did you pick up in the deli?"

"Girl, you ain't ready for me."

"What? What?"

"I'm not even ready for me."

"Well are you gonna tell me sometime today," asked Kayla, anxiously?

"Alright, I'm working up to it."

"Well, get to it, will you! We ain't as young as we used to be."

"Okay, here goes. I met a man," I quickly blurted out, then closed my eyes to avoid Kayla's judgmental facial expressions, I just knew she was making.

"You met a man?" she asked. I imagined her with raised eyebrows, almost touching her hairline. "What man?"

"A fine man; he was in his work get-up though, all covered in dirt."

"Reina, what are you doing out meeting men, especially while you're still with Lance and double especially when he's covered in dirt, what the hell?"

"It just happened."

"Damn Reina; tell me all about him."

"Not much to tell really... ooh girl I'm lying... He was so cute, fine, a gentleman, and girl, he can cook too."

"Cook, well maybe now you'll be relieved of your kitchen duties that you tend to abandon anyway."

"Don't make jokes. This is serious."

"What's so serious about it? Lighten up!"

"How can I? I'm nervous about our date on Friday."

"Date, Oh my God. Isn't that a little soon?"

"It's a little late if you ask me."

"What are you going to do about Lance? You know how possessive he is. You better keep this on the down low for now," said Kayla.

"Do you think I'm simple or something Kayla? I got it under control. Don't worry about it."

"So what's up? Where is your date going to be?"

"We're supposed to be getting together Friday evening at his house. He's cooking me dinner."

"Mmm, what is he making, every guy's usual, spaghetti?"

"Actually, he's cooking some fancy dish, something about beef cooked in a wine sauce."

"Get out!"

"I know. I'm so excited," I said, showing all thirty-two of my teeth. "I haven't been out with anybody besides Lance in three and a half years."

"Maybe because you've been married for the past three years, ya think?"

"Ha ha, very funny,"

"I can't believe you. What are you going to do about Lance? You can't juggle them both. Lance won't be having that, girlfriend."

"Thank you for your concern Ms. Thing, but I'll figure something out."

"If you say so,"

"I say so. I just need some time to think, that's all."

"Well just be careful, whatever you decide."

"What if I dump Lance and this guy turns out to be a jerk, which I doubt, but you never know?"

"Then you just go out there to the pond and catch you another fish. It's not like you want to be with Lance anymore, anyway. You and I can go out to a nice jazz set or to hear the spoken word one night and see what happens, you game for that?"

"I don't know Kay. I've been with him for a while. I guess I'm just used to him. Besides that, he pays all of my bills and gets my hair and my nails done every week. Who am I going to get to take his place so soon?"

"Reina, don't you have a job?"

"Of course I have a job, so what?"

"So, go get your own hair and nails done."

"What? Girl I wouldn't hardly know what it's like to not have a man pay for my beauty treatments. Besides, do you know how expensive facials and massages are these days?"

"Forget the beauty regimen, what about your bills? Do you think you can handle them on your own?"

"Well if I absolutely had to Kayla, but I don't want to, that's the whole point. There wouldn't be anything left after bills. If you haven't noticed, I live a lavish lifestyle. Whoever gets with me is going to have to maintain it."

"Yes indeed. I know it'll be somewhat of a struggle to have to pay your own way, but what's more important, having a man who pays all your bills and you're unhappy, or paying your own bills and having peace of mind?"

"You want the politically correct answer is to that question? Girl listen, I just like it when men pamper me and treat me like a princess."

"You are a princess Reina. You are just so used to brothers paying your bills, taking you shopping and buying you things that it's a little bit intimidating for you to even think of doing it yourself. Personally, I can't relate to that. I wish I had a guy to take me on shopping sprees; instead I got stuck with Luther. But oh well, can't win them all." Kayla chuckled.

"Yeah but Kay, you have cash budding on the trees in your backyard. I don't have that. All I have is a pretty face and a banging body to match. Men want to take care of me. I can't help that, can I?"

"Just remember, all of that stuff comes with a price."

"Exactly, and this is why I never allowed myself to get too emotionally attached to anyone, except Lance. I guess that's why it bothers me so much that he does not trust me, because I completely let my guard down with him."

"Are you scared to be on your own Reina?"

"Girl, I'm terrified. I'm scared of all of the responsibilities that go along with living alone. A mortgage, light bill, water bill, home phone bill, digital cable bill, internet service, cell phone, groceries, and that's not including my personal hygiene products or my lunch dates with you. What if I don't make enough money to cover everything?"

"But you will Reina, if you sacrifice a few shopping sprees and a few hair-dos. You'll be fine. I'll even help you set up a budget. We'll sit down together and work it out, okay?"

"Well, I guess it's gonna have to be, since you're pressuring me to leave Lance like... today," I said, sarcastically.

"Well excuse me. Sometimes you make bad decisions so I'm just trying to help keep you from getting your butt kicked."

"I hear you girl, thanks. Talk to you later."

"Okay, bye," said Kayla.

I hung up the phone. I had a lot to think about. Kayla had a point. I just didn't want to admit it. She has always been the responsible one. Well, for the most part. She's the crazy, responsible type, if there is any such thing.

The chicken sat frozen in its package. That meant I had a while to myself before I had to play the role of Martha Stewart. I lay down on the couch and closed my eyes. It was meditation time. I reached over to the end table to retrieve my eye pillow to help me relax a little.

I heard a noise that startled me. I must have overslept. I jumped up abruptly. Lance walked in the door, carrying his black leather Kenneth Cole briefcase. We still had not resolved our issues from the night before.

"Hey what's up baby doll?" Lance asked, enthusiastically.

"Hey," I replied dryly, rubbing my eyes.

"Oh, I'm so hungry I could eat...you," said Lance, smiling at me.

I couldn't help looking at him in disgust. Why doesn't he get a backbone and stop being so doggone nice all of the time? Maybe I would respect him more. I don't want him to be abusive but show me who the man is around here, damn.

"Where's my dinner babe?" Lance asked, as he sat on the couch beside me putting his feet up on the coffee table.

"I'm on my way to fix it right now."

"You mean you don't have anything ready yet?" Lance asked, at a complete loss.

"Not yet," I responded, in a not-so-nice tone.

The smile on Lance's face just dissolved and all of his facial features became gathered into a scowl. He came from a family where his mother cooked a big breakfast in the morning, packed all of their lunches, and had a five-course meal ready at the same time every evening.

Lance's father always said the blessing, and then they ate together while discussing events from everyone's day. Lance was an only child, which would explain him being spoiled, which he denies. At least, I know I'm spoiled. I can admit it too. Two spoiled brats living under the same roof can be annoying. Somehow, we have managed to co-exist together, until now.

"How could you not have dinner ready, Reina? It's almost nine o'clock at night. I worked all day then went over to help my boy out with his car so that he can get back and forth to work to be able to support his family and I come home to nothing to eat? What have you been doing all day?" Lance yelled, angrily.

Oh my God, he knows something, I thought to myself.

"I accidentally fell asleep, Lance. Anyway why can't you ever cook dinner?"

"I'll tell you why. When you see an outfit you like, who do you ask to buy it for you? When you need your hair and nails done who pays for that? When you don't have enough cash to pay on your credit card bills, who pays on them? When your broke ass can't afford to go out on the weekends to the club with your girlfriends, you come to who? That's right Reina, don't be shy. Speak up please. Lance can I have thirty, forty, fifty dollars so my girls don't have to buy my drinks all night. Does any of this sound familiar Reina? I always make sure you're alright. You fixing my dinner is only doing your part. That's why, but its okay if you feel like I'm asking too much of you. Just make sure you don't ask too much of me from now on!" Lance barked, with raised eyebrows.

Wow, he had me. He got mad and read me like a book. That's what I'm talking about. Read me baby! Do not let me walk all over you. I liked it when Lance stood up to me. It made me feel like I was with a strong man. What woman wants a little weak, timid, whinny-butt for a man? Not me.

Because of my physical appearance guys always fall at my feet, kind of like they did Jesus in the biblical days, so it's kind of refreshing when a guy doesn't take my crap.

You go boy, I thought to myself. Put your foot down! I couldn't think of anything else to say so I just kept it simple. "Lance, I simply fell asleep. Can't you understand that?" I asked.

"Reina, I would understand if it only happened once or twice, even a few times but this happens every other day. You couldn't cook because of this or that but here you come with your hands out for money. I can't even get any love-making when I want it. It's always on your terms. Let me tell you something babe. You better get it together."

I just put my head in my lap. I knew he was right, but my pride wouldn't let me give him the satisfaction. Therefore, I kept up the argument a little while longer so I didn't appear weak.

Lance picked up the telephone, dialed a number, and then spoke in a low tone.

"Hey, what's happening sweetie? Oh, I'm all right, just starving. What did you cook? Mmm, that sounds delicious. Put a plate on the side for me, I'm on my way over," Lance hung up the phone and put his shoes back on.

"Where do you think you're going?" I asked.

"I don't think I'm going anywhere. I know exactly where I'm going," said Lance, as he picked up the phone to erase the number he had just dialed.

"Well, where would that be?" I asked, in a panic.

You would think that after how we had been getting along lately I should be glad to see him go. Even though I didn't want him anymore, I couldn't bear the thought of him being with anyone else, typical.

"Don't wait up", he slammed the door behind him.

"Where could he be going?" I asked myself.

I walked over to the caller ID box to see if he really erased the number he called, and sure enough, he had.

I couldn't believe Lance would be so bold as to call another woman from my house, erase the number then go over to her house to eat her food and tell me not to wait up. How dare he disrespect me like that? How dare he? I wondered if it was the girl from the Fourth of July party. I didn't see them exchange numbers, but then again I turned away from them so he wouldn't think I was watching him. Well if he wants to play this game with me, so be it, I thought to myself. May the best man or shall I say woman win.

I picked my purse up from the floor where I had thrown it earlier, dug, and dug until I found Kenny's number. I looked at it for about ten minutes trying to build up the nerve to call him. I just sat there depicting everything about his name and phone number on that little piece of paper.

"Hello?" sounded a deep voice, sending chills down my spine.

For a minute I could not speak. The thought of talking to another man behind Lance's back hit me, all at once. I felt overwhelmed with guilt.

"Hello," the voice said again.

"Hi, uh, Kenny," I said, nervously.

My confidence was not exuding and I felt helpless. What am I doing? I couldn't believe I was about to be unfaithful for the very first time. I was actually planning to be unfaithful. This was so premeditated. I knew I was going to give it up to Kenny from the moment I saw him at the deli, oh my God! Am I a horrible person? I asked myself.

"Yes, this is Kenny. Who is this?" he asked.

I started to hang up but something led me not to.

"This is Reina. You met me at...." Before I could finish my statement, Kenny interjected.

"Yes, yes, hey Reina. How are you?" he asked, pleasantly surprised.

"Oh, I'm fine, thank you. I just thought I'd give you a call today and maybe set something up for tomorrow evening," I said, apprehensively.

"That sounds good. What did you have in mind? Is there anything in particular or would you prefer if I did all of the planning? I'd love to handle things for us if you don't mind," said Kenny, taking control.

Thank you Jesus, a man after my own heart... and he cooks too? I couldn't get over that part. Lance couldn't even boil water. Every time he tries to boil an egg he always forgets about it, all of the water boils out of the pot, and it scorches leaving a very bad smell in the house, not to mention what happens to the poor little egg.

"Yeah, why don't you handle things this time and I'll follow in your footsteps for the next time," I said.

"No problem, baby girl," Kenny endearingly spoke.

Oh my God, he called me baby. Those words sounded so good rolling off his lips. Oh my God, I could just lie down and have his children right now. I'm in love... already.

"Okay then, see you tomorrow Kenny." I said, hesitantly, trying to s-t-r-e-t-c-h my words out a little longer. I did not want the conversation to end, but I did not know when Lance was going to walk back through the door.

"Bye, baby girl."

He did it again. I thought I was going to pass out and then die. I thought I could leave Lance's greedy butt that night and run straight into the arms of my new love but I knew it was best to take it slow. After all, I had only seen him once. I didn't want to seem desperate, even though I probably was.

"Bye," I said, and then we hung up.

As soon as I put the phone down it began to ring again. That's probably Lance calling to apologize, I thought, as I picked it up.

"Hello," I answered.

"Hey baby girl, it's me Kenneth."

I almost dropped the phone. I couldn't believe he called my house number back. I must have forgotten to block my number. Lance is gonna go off. Oh my God! We'll all be six feet under, stinking somewhere.

"Hey Kenny," I said, with a shaken voice.

"I forgot to give you my address," he said, in good spirits.

"Okay, what is it?" I rushed.

"Thirty-seven thirty-five Mount Coving Drive. It's near the...."

"I know where it is. See you tomorrow Kenny, I have to go," I said swiftly and hung up the phone as fast as I could without hanging up in his face.

I really didn't know where it was, but I had to avoid a long drawn out explanation. I could just go on-line and look it up on map quest. I didn't even tell him not to call again.

I rushed over to where the caller ID sat on the coffee table and erased Kenny's number. The very first thing Lance does when he gets home is head straight for the phone. Sometimes he calls the numbers back and asks if anyone called for Lance or Reina. Geez, I should have blocked my number before I called Kenny. What was I thinking? Now what am I going to do? My mind was so boggled. I didn't want to tell Kenny not to call because I don't want him to know I am married, at least not yet. He might not want me if he knew I was involved with another guy. He might figure it's too much trouble to be bothered with all of the drama that usually goes along with that, but I had to do something.

I heard the keys jingling in the door. Lance had arrived back home. I looked over at the clock to see how late it was so I could have some dirt on him but it was only nine-thirty.

"Hey babe, I'm home. I just want to let you know that I don't think we should go to bed angry. I went to my mother's house. You know she cooks every day. That's where I always go when you don't cook. I didn't want to tell you that though because you always tease me about being a big mama's boy," Lance said.

Lord Jesus, he made me think he was going over to another woman's house. Ugh! I should have known. Lance is no player. He just pretended to be one when I acted up and I called Kenny thinking...ugh. Where's my rock? This time when I crawl under my rock, I am going to stay there.

# Chapter 10

The doorbell sounded. Damn! I was sleeping so well, too.

"What time is it?" I groggily said aloud. I looked up at the clock on the wall, "seven o clock! Who in the world would be at my door at seven o clock in the morning?" I stumbled over my Chanel sandals, trying to grab my silk robe that I had thrown on the Victorian chaise lounge before bed last night. I finally made it to the door, looked through the peephole and there she stood, four feet two inches. Her hair pulled back in a ponytail with a few curls hanging from her temples, dressed in her Girl Scout get up, holding boxes of cookies, smiling from ear to ear, looking in the direction of the peephole.

The nerve, I thought. What's wrong with these people? I guess they think that everyone should be awake at seven am. Well, I'm a kept woman. I don't have to work, unless of course I want to. My little part time job doesn't require my presence until noon. How dare she knock on my door this early! She's lucky she's just a little kid or I would give her a piece of my mind.

The bell rang again and Rose was already standing next to me, all of six inches tall, barking her bold and saucy bark, waiting for me to open the door.

"Good morning. My name is Sarah and I'm selling Girl Scout cookies", she said.

"Duh," I thought, as I smiled and tried my best not to go off on this little girl with the Green Beret.

"Well how nice," I whispered, trying to maintain my phony smile.

"Would you like to buy a box?" Sarah politely asked, smiling, showing all twelve of her teeth.

"Sure. I'll take a box of the thin mint," I said, as I went to get a ten-dollar bill out of my Prada bag.

We finished our transaction and I headed back to my big luxurious empty bed where I slid gently under the goose down comforter and covered my eyes with my silk, lavender scented eye pillow. Lance had already left for work, so I could finally enjoy having the whole bed to myself, nobody to yank the covers over to one side until I am completely uncovered; nobody snoring so loudly that I can't hear what the people in my dreams are talking about and last but not least, no stench of boiled eggs when I raise the covers up to turn from one side to the other. "Yessss," I said, aloud. "Back to la la land I go. This is the life."

Then out of nowhere, it hit me. "Oh my God," I screamed, sitting up quickly in the bed, as if I had just abruptly awakened from a bad dream. Today is the day I planned to go over to Kenny's house for dinner. I had to pick out something incredible to wear. I had a million things to do. I had to be stunning. Where was I going to tell Lance I was going? He probably wouldn't be there to notice I was gone anyway. I knew I should probably go to the salon to get my hair flat ironed. Maybe an up-do would be nice and elegant. Then again, I did meet him in shabby work clothes. I didn't know what his style was. He might not even like elegant. My mind was going a mile a minute. I needed to breathe. In through the nose and out through the mouth. In through the nose and out through the mouth. Count to ten! Relax girl! Oh my, I was talking to myself again. I thought I should have some herbal tea and a nice hot bubble bath by candlelight, while listening to my Will Downing CD, all by myself, as usual, to calm me down. I needed to get a life. This wining and dining myself thing was lonely sometimes, but it would have to do for now. It was actually better if I was alone anyway, so I could fantasize about my baby Kenny in peace. Look at me, claiming the boy already. Now you know, I had to stop the madness.

After considering all of what would be involved in getting ready for my date, I decided to cut my sleep short and start preparing for my romantic rendezvous. I needed to work on my lie. Tonight would be the perfect night to do it too, because Lance and I never made up from our fight, although I should have been the one to apologize. Instead, I could use the argument as an excuse to get me out of the house. I could say that I needed some time alone to myself to think, and that I did not want to argue anymore, so I was going out with the girls tonight, to clear my head. That was if he caught me before I left the house. When he called my cell phone, I would just tell him that I was at Kayla's house and I may not be coming home tonight and I might not, depending on how things went with Kenny. I knew my girl Kayla would cover for me. That's just how the game goes. Friends cover for one another, no matter what.

I jumped out of bed, placed my meditation tape in the player, then sat on the posh carpet of my bedroom floor and began my kundalini yoga routine, which required stretching, breathing, chanting mantras and meditating. After a full hour of grounding myself, I put my flowered plastic shower cap on to take a shower. I didn't want to get my hair wet because I may have opted to get some honey blonde highlights later, just a few to frame my face.

I thought I would settle for just having my hair and nails done today. I would normally get a massage, but I'm hoping Kenny will offer to give me one and in that case, I didn't want to be sore from one of Jarvis' deep tissue massages. I wanted my whole body to be sensitive to

Kenny's every touch. I did not want anybody else's fingerprints on me before I saw him. I wanted to be pure and untouched, like a virgin when he touched me for the very first time. I knew I was being presumptuous, but I anticipated having Kenny's hands all over me all throughout the night.

I went into the kitchen to make myself a cup of hot herbal tea, when I noticed the cappuccino maker was still on. Lance must have left it on for me, so I had that instead. I took my coffee mug with me into the library so that I could read my e-mails. Gina sent me one saying how much she enjoyed our visit but it was too short lived.

There were a few others, even one from Lance. He likes to send me e-mails all throughout the day, saying little sweet nothings. Under normal circumstances, I would be more receptive to Lance's attempts to have cyber sex, but I was not feeling him right then, at all.

I had not been to work in almost a week, so I called. Ms. Charlene said that business was still slow this week, so I could take the day off, if I wanted to. I wanted to feel like I was still being productive, even though I was not there in person, so I placed a few textile orders while I was already at the computer.

At least I didn't have to clean the house before I slipped out of there later. Maggie, our housekeeper who comes once a week had already swept and mopped the floors, vacuumed the carpet, dusted the furniture, wiped down the blinds and changed the bed linens. I don't know what I would do without her. She's a Godsend. Lance knew I wasn't domestic when he met me. Now all of a sudden he wants to turn me into Heidi, the happy homemaker.

I went into our walk-in closet to get an idea of what I wanted to wear for Kenny tonight. Guys never know how much effort women put into looking good for them. I had hoped he would appreciate it. I was sure he would. He seemed like the appreciative type. I ran across a couple of nice choices, but did not concretely decide on anything. The one outfit though that stood out to me was my Apple-bottom strapless jumpsuit. It was certainly an eye-catcher.

I put my clothes on, hopped in the car, plugged in my I pod, chose a song and headed eastbound to the salon. On the fifteen-minute drive to Metairie, I called Kayla from my cell phone to alert her of my plan, which I had not thoroughly devised yet. I'd hoped that maybe she had some ideas to help me out. Knowing her, she would be full of them.

I returned home after visiting the salon, looked in the bedroom mirror and tried to perfect my already perfect french twist. I made a quick call to Lance to figure out his whereabouts. He seemed vague, as if he knew I had a motive. I tried my best to sound normal. Maybe men have a strong intuition like women do. Nah, I was probably just paranoid.

The plan that I worked out was, I was spending the night over at Kayla's house and I would be home sometime the next day, late morning. That way, I could stay over at Kenny's house as long as I wanted. We could even see the sunrise together if we wanted to. It was going to be grand; I could feel it.

The time had come. I packed my little overnight bag that held all of my feminine products, my special soaps that I liked to bathe with along with my bath puff, shampoo, and conditioner. A toothbrush... toothpaste... mouthwash, white strips and waxed floss, deodorant, my double edged razor, my cleansing facial wash, moisturizing lotion, my Mac make-up kit, scented body lotion, my Gucci perfume, tampons and thong panty liners...cause you never know, condoms....just in case and a douche. That should cover it.

I headed on over to Kenny's house. I was so excited I could hardly wait to see him. I felt like a little school girl all over again.

I opened the door to the garage, making sure that Lance had not parked in there, without me noticing him. Then I looked out of the window to see if he was sitting out in front of the house dilly-dallying in his glove compartment, as he so often does. He was not, so off I went.

I vigilantly headed out of the front door in a hurry, stepped over the Times Picayune newspaper, which laid in the walkway. I got into my car and screeched off down the street. One of my neighbors, old Mrs. Johnson was watering her daisies out front. Her upper arm jiggled as she waved to me when I drove off. I pushed the button to let the top down. I wasn't worried about my hair since Enrique sprayed it to death. I slid my Jill Scott CD into the player and began enjoying her whimsical lyrics, as the car cruised at the speed of seventy miles per hour. I decided to ride the ferry across the river to help ease my anxiety. I reached the main street that would lead me straight to Kenny's house. I grabbed my compact out of my purse to brush some bronzer across my already golden cheeks, touched up my hair in the rear view mirror, slid my wedding ring off my finger and put it in the glove compartment. I talked to myself, as I always do when I'm nervous. I coached myself on what I was going to say when he opened the door, and what initial pose I was going to strike to catch his attention and how I was going to behave. I wanted his first impression of me to be perfect. I made it to the house finally. After so much anticipation, I was finally there.

I was actually surprised to see what a cute little house he had with a neatly cut yard and quite a few potted plants hanging on his porch. There was also a wooden swing, small enough to seat two people, barely, but I was sure we could squeeze in there together when the time was right. All I needed was him, to be a willing participant. A big bay window allowed me to see straight into his well-organized sunroom.

I rang the bell after standing at the door, assessing my surroundings. I checked the house out from top to bottom. I noticed things about this house that I didn't know I knew. He needed to clean his gutters and a few shingles were missing from the roof. Lord, when did I learn about gutters and shingles? I fidgeted with the straps of my cotton candy pink halter dress, which perfectly matched my nail color. I heard the sounds of his footsteps make its way to the sunroom to open the door. There he stood: tall, and effortlessly handsome. He looked so different from when I saw him at the deli. If I didn't know any better, I would think I knocked on the wrong door. This guy standing there in front of me was breathtaking. I knew it had to be some reason why I was so taken aback by this grimy looking guy in the store. He certainly cleaned up well.

"Hi Reina," Kenny said, smiling from ear to ear.

"Hey Kenny, How are you?" I gleamed, trying not to seem as excited as I really was.

"Well come on in," he said, with opened arms, silently offering me a hug.

We embraced and I slowly followed his lead as he walked me from the front door into the living room. The house smelled of opium incense burning and there was reggae music softly playing in the background. The house was spotless. I wondered if he had a housekeeper or if he did the cleaning himself.

"Have a seat here on the sofa, Reina. Please make yourself at home."

By the time he offered for me to make myself at home I had already taken my shoes off and they were sitting nice and neat, right next to my feet.

"Thank you Kenny. That's very sweet of you."

"May I get you something to drink?"

"Sure. Do you have red wine?"

"I wouldn't be caught dead without it."

"Kind of like me. That's how I feel about my credit cards."

We both chuckled, while discreetly looking each other over. I could feel the attraction that we had for one another, but I pretended not to notice, as I privately did my kegel exercises.

Kenny went to pour me a glass of red wine. I looked him up and down as he walked over to his wet bar. I liked watching him move. He was so graceful, the way he took such soft footsteps when he walked. The way he tilted the glass, as he slowly poured the wine. He looked me directly in the eyes when he spoke to me from across the room. He wore his sterling silver rings on his middle fingers and a hoop earring in each ear. His jeans cut off at the bottom, starting to shred and slightly sagged in the back. Only the bottom half of his straight white teeth showed when he spoke. He crossed his legs when he sat and ran his fingers through his dreads as he listened to me talk. His voice, the choice of words he used, everything about him...I could not stop admiring him. What odd things I noticed about him. He was very different from what I thought he would be. I mean, I knew he would turn out to be worth keeping, but I didn't know he was going to be so fascinating. Just looking around his house, as he gave me the tour was amazing. He had such eclectic taste. Some would call him eccentric, but I found him to be intriguing.

"Tell me a little bit about yourself Reina. What's your favorite color?"

"Hmm, I like pink."

"Really, I guess I should have known that huh?"

"How?"

"Uh, you're wearing a pink dress." We chuckled.

"My turn, what's your favorite television show?"

"Oh, that's easy, The Simpson's."

"The Simpson's, why is that?"

"I don't know. That show just cracks me up."

He laughed excitedly, as if he had a flashback from one of the episodes. Oh my Lord, the man likes The Simpson's.

"Okay, my turn...hmm, what's your favorite...I don't know...flower?"

"Rose,"

"Don't you need more time to think of an answer, you just blurted it out like, I like roses? Is that a hint?"

"Awe, you got jokes, huh?" I laughed.

Kenny made fun of me and we laughed some more.

"Would you like to see the rest of the place Reina, or would you rather just sit and drink your wine?"

"Sure I would, absolutely."

Kenny handed me a glass of Cabernet Sauvignon and we walked through the rest of the house. Kenny had original pieces of art that hanged, or sat on plinths all throughout his living quarters. Each one of them autographed. I was impressed with his love for the African culture. Each of the rooms in Kenny's house had a touch of brilliance. In the master bedroom, there were delicately handcrafted statues, with many intricate details of all sizes that sat in their designated places. It looked as if he put a lot of thought into placing them in the perfect spots. Hanging on a mount above the dresser were two African fighting spears. On an empty wall, leading into the master bath was a black mask that someone carved from an Mpingo tree and wore in a Tanzanian spear fight. Out of the corner of my eye, I happened to notice the bow and arrow, encased in a tall glass cabinet that sat cattycorner to the left of the room. Then there were the paintings. I thought the ones in the Great room were enchanting, but the thirty by forty inch mind-blower, positioned right above his king sized water bed had completely captured my full undivided attention, for at least a good ten minutes. I couldn't take my eyes off of it. I intently stared into the eyes of all of the members of the tribe of Masai, as they stared directly back at me. Kenny seemed as interested in telling me all about the painting, as I was to hear about it. He did not seem like he was tired of talking about it, even though I knew he had to go through this same routine every time someone new saw it. There was no way that he should ever get tired of looking at it or talking about it. It was such a passionate piece. I had vivid dreams about it at night. He said that the guy that painted it was still a lively tribe member and he paints for food, to feed his ailing wife and seven kids.

Kenny said the artists name was Uchenna. What was so amazing was how he painted it just as he saw it. Uchenna sat back, watched his tribal members interact with one another, and captured it on cardboard. He captured images of his over worked wife washing her dress in a metal tin outside of their one room straw hut with dirt floors, while three of his boys wearing torn shorts only, playfully wrestled one another to the ground. One of his daughters danced gracefully, while the other two sang and clapped their hands. The baby boy clung himself tightly around one of his mother's swollen legs, as his cloth diaper hung loosely around his waist. In addition, there were other people vaguely faded in the background.

"Kenny, this is all so intense. I can hardly catch my breath."

"Thank you Reina. I enjoy all of my pieces individually. They all have their own special meanings to me."

"Wow! But what is your fascination with Africa?"

"Well, as a teenager I was an exchange student and was fortunate enough to find a really nice family to live with in Africa for a whole year. Then I was an African American Studies major in college and..."

"Oh, you went to college?" I asked, cutting him off in mid sentence.

"Most definitely, you seem surprised!"

"Well, no... Not really," I lied.

"Anyway, I became interested in African American studies in college."

"Did you graduate?"

"It's straight to the nitty gritty for you, huh?"

"Well I'm just curious. It'll help me to know how to... interact with you better."

"Are you serious?"

"Well... Yeah, most people that didn't attend college are..."

"Are what?"

"Never mind,"

"But I'm interested in hearing your view point."

"I'd really rather not talk about this. I tend to offend black people with my view point on this matter."

"Aren't you black Reina?"

"Yes, but I don't have that typical black woman's welfare mentality."

"Now you have to tell me! Come on Reina."

"Well, if you went to college I feel that you are better educated than the common brother on many levels, therefore I can speak to you in my normal manner without feeling like..."

"Like what?"

"Like I need to downplay my education for you to be able to better relate to me."

"Just be yourself sister, that's all."

"I will. Maybe I'm jumping the gun a little, but I just like to know what I'm dealing with."

"That's understandable. Do you have something against brothers who don't attend college?"

"I am just so tired of those brothers who talk about the white man this and the white man that. Always talking about how the white man has held them back. They would rather be selling drugs on the corner somewhere than to pick up a book. I just don't get it. I think if they tried just as hard, they could have damn near the same opportunities, maybe not all, but a lot. The world is changing. There are many opportunities for blacks now."

"Have you ever been discriminated against Reina?"

"I can't think of anything off hand, but even if I had, I can't let that stop me from doing what I have to do. Sometimes you have to take matters into your own hands and create your own opportunities."

"Have you ever gone in for a job and went up against a white applicant, who was not nearly as qualified as you and he landed the position instead of you?" asked Kenny.

"I don't know. I never paid much attention to that, I guess," I responded.

"How about a loan, have you ever applied for a loan and had the same amount of collateral as a white person and you were denied?" Kenny queried.

"I've never needed a loan. I've always used cash to purchase whatever I wanted," I responded, defensively.

"Do you know anybody that committed a misdemeanor and it was celebrated by the media, as if it was a felony and when your white neighbor Jacob actually did commit a felony, that story received no attention at all?"

"Actually, no; are you talking about somebody you know? It sounds like these scenarios are near and dear to your heart," I said.

"As a matter of fact, I am. I went up for a position at this reputable corporation against one of my colleagues, of the Caucasian persuasion, whose credentials were not as impressive as mine and was told that I had been beat out by someone better suited for the position. The CEO of the company didn't realize that Nick and I knew each other from college. I guess it was somewhat of an experiment on my part, because I already knew what would happen. Nick felt bad because even he knew I should've gotten that job, but needless to say he didn't resign.

Secondly, my same partner Nick applied for a loan at the exact bank that I did and managed to receive one while having an outstanding balance of a hundred thousand dollars in student loans while I attended school on a basketball scholarship. I didn't have any debt. Neither of us had any collateral but guess who was awarded a loan, for thirty thousand dollars?

Last, but not least, my boy Mohammed was driving down the street smoking marijuana and got pulled over for an expired license plate. The police officer smelled the weed and asked him to step out of the car, pointing a glock twenty-two at him. The officer got on the radio and the next thing you know, there were about five back up vehicles. They tore up the entire interior in his car, doing what they called a routine search and found nothing. They ran his name... nothing. Mohammed fully complied with the officers commands but was still taken to jail for possession of a third of a joint. Meanwhile, Jacob who lived three houses down from me swindled almost a quarter of a million dollars from the company that he still works for, with only a consequence of attending a year's worth of counseling sessions and having to pay the money back a little at a time, from each of his paychecks. He said he needed the money to pay off some of his debts that he and his wife had incurred over the years. They let him off with only an insignificant punishment but Mohammed ended up in handcuffs. Now you tell me Reina who the real thugs are?" Kenny said, sighing as if he were glad to have gotten that off his chest.

I felt helpless. I had to catch myself from drooling. My mouth was wide open, as if I were waiting to catch flies. I was mesmerized at how conscious this brother really was. I was even more turned on than before.

"Come with me please!" he insisted, leading me back into the Great room.

Kenny walked to his built in bookshelf, anxiously searching for a book that he evidently wanted me to thumb through. He found it, turned to a certain chapter, and handed it to me. Was he kidding? I am trying to get my drink on and get close to him a little bit and he wants me to read a book. I could see if it was a romance novel or something but I was not in the mood for a history lesson. I was beginning to realize, this brother was going to be a tough nut to crack. He was deep.

"Read a little bit of this Reina. I think it will help you understand our history a little bit better. You really need some awareness on our people and how we were slaves, for many years and yes, there are more opportunities for us now, but slavery and prejudice are not over by a long shot. We are not free."

I took the book, *Life on the Old Plantation in Ante-Bellum Days*, and glanced through it. There was so much informative reading. I quickly became overwhelmed. I sat with my head immersed in the pages, skimming for about fifteen minutes, took a deep breath and looked up at the ceiling to clear my head a little, since it was spinning.

"Well, what do you think now?"

"Sure enough our ancestors had it hard, being enslaved and all, but that was then, this is now. Times have changed."

"I know it seems like times have changed Reina, but believe me, they haven't changed all that much."

"We aren't enslaved anymore; we've been emancipated, at a snail's pace, but nonetheless..."

"Ohhhh, but I beg to differ. Our minds are still enslaved. We are subtly taught everyday how not to love ourselves and to feel inferior to the white race. The media plays a big part in sending us subliminal messages. That's why you must know who you really are, so that you are not taken in by the manipulation. Think about it!"

"Okay, I will. I promise, I'll think about it."

Time seemed to be moving at a rapid pace and the romantic atmosphere was slowly slipping away. Kenny appeared intuitive to the shift in my mood, so he changed the subject and I was delighted.

"On a lighter note, how's your wine Reina?"

"It's really good, with a grip, just the way I like it."

"Hmm, a wine connoisseur, huh?"

"I know a little something," I said, modestly, as I let the flavor seduce my palate.

"Would you like to listen to some music other than what I have playing?"

"No way, I love Bob Marley; Bob was the man."

"Oh, so you know about Bob too?"

"Yeah, I know he smoked a lot of weed."

"There's a whole lot more to him than that though."

"Oh, I'm sure; I'm just being silly."

We had wonderful conversations as the night went on. This man knew a little bit about everything, it seemed, particularly when it came to his heritage. I hung on to his every word. At some points, I was so hypnotized watching his lips move, that I completely tuned everything else in the room out, even what he was saying. I couldn't help it. I think he knew when I zoned out because he would stop talking and just look at me.

"So Reina, tell me more about yourself."

"What do you want to know, anything in particular?"

"Uh, just start at the beginning," Kenny said, smiling.

I was hoping he didn't start asking questions that I would have to evade or downright lie about, one or the two, so I just started talking about my hobbies, my likes, and dislikes.

Before I knew it, time had flown away. It was already nine-thirty.

"Are you ready to eat yet, Reina?"

"Actually, I have worked up an appetite."

"Okay. You sit right there and I'll go fix us a plate."

"Why don't you let me help you Kenny? I don't mind."

"If you insist, you can come with me, but I really don't need any help fixing the plates. Just sit there and look pretty."

He had better hurry up and give me my food. Otherwise, I may just have to eat him. He said the sweetest things.

I had ever seen a man's kitchen fully equipped like Kenny's, mostly because he was a bachelor. This man had everything. His ex-wife must have been a very thorough person. He even had things that I don't have in my kitchen, like a waffle maker and a fondue set. Lance took it upon himself to buy me every kitchen utensil on the market, in hopes that one day I would become domestic, ha! I swear sometimes I think that man is on crack. Kenny even had a George Forman grill, a juicer, smoothie machine, bread maker, steamer, crock-pot, blender, rice cooker, and a wok. I also spotted a large collection of stainless steel pots and pans when he opened the freshly stained wooden cabinets to put one of them away.

As I was appreciating all of the trouble he had gone through for our date, his cell phone chirped.

"Hello," he answered. "Heyyy baby", he said, in a whispered tone. Yeah, I received it today... thanks a lot...just about to sit down and eat...talk to you tomorrow...good night...me too."

I heard the whole conversation, but couldn't figure out who he was talking to. Whoever it was, he called them baby. That was the same thing he called me. I didn't like that, at all. I did not want to let on that I was somewhat jealous right then, because it was too soon for that. He might think I was a lunatic or something. I guess now I had to make it through this dinner without showing my true feelings. Even though this was only our first date, I wanted to feel like his only woman tonight.

Kenny hung up the phone and did not say a word to me about who he was talking to and I didn't dare ask. He grabbed my hand and escorted me a few feet to the left of the kitchen, into the dining area to sit down and eat. Kenny dimmed the lights into a soft rosy hue, and then served me my dinner on one of the prettiest pieces of real china that matched the other dishes on the table. I was truly impressed now. He went to get our wine from the other room, and then sat across from me. I was hoping that we would sit side by side while eating. I felt the need to be close to him, but I did not want to say anything. I didn't want to seem like I was complaining about something so trivial as the seating arrangements, so I pretended not to be high maintenance at that moment and try to just relish in the opportunity of being in his company, period.

"Mmm, Kenny this looks delicious. I'm not kidding."

"Let's hope it tastes as good as it looks," Kenny said, being humble again.

It smelled fantastic, and when I put that first bite of succulent beef into my mouth, it was almost as if I was ingesting Kenny instead. I knew I deserved the royal treatment like this. Kenny certainly knew how to treat a lady, that's for sure. I knew he would. I could just tell from the first day I spotted him in the crowded delicatessen.

"It's amazing, simply amazing," I said, as I slowly tried to chew the recommended thirty two times to aid in better digestion. Ahh... who am I kidding, I was just being bourgeois.

"You like?" he asked.

"I love," I responded.

We sat there and finished our dinner, listening to the dulcet sounds that protruded through the speakers that were in the ceiling in every room of the house. Time continued to fly by. It was time to cuddle or... something. He had not touched me all night. I was beginning to get worried. Did he find me attractive? I wouldn't be at his house if he didn't. He was not gay because he would have inquired about my male siblings by now. What was his deal? Maybe he was just trying to be respectable. Maybe he was waiting on me to make the first move. Yeah, that's it. That was just what I would do. I would make an ever so smooth move on him.

We made our way back into the original room to continue listening to his versatile collection of music, which was mostly reggae and neo-soul. By that time, we had heard Bob Marley, Steel Pulse, Erica Badu, India Irie and Lauren Hill among a few other artists. Kenny sat on the far left end of his orchid white dual reclining loveseat. I tried to scoot in closer to him while trying not to be obvious, as usual, when I was being sly.

"Thank you for a wonderful dinner, Kenny."

"You are more than welcome, Reina."

"What do you want to do now?" I asked, while giving him sweet eyes.

"Well, I don't want to cut our night short because I'm truly enjoying your company but I do have a doctor's appointment in the morning."

Now I knew he was not trying to put me out before he gave me some affection. I was not ready to go yet. Okay, I was going to have to step it up a notch for him. He obviously couldn't read body language very well. Maybe he was a little slow. I was going to have to do something extreme to turn him on.

I crossed my right leg over my left, dangling my cotton-candy colored painted toes, which sat flawlessly in my Gucci mule sandals, to expose my butterfly tattoo, gently against his pant leg. When he looked away, I slid my tank top down a little more to show more cleavage. I took one of the fringed accent pillows and placed it on my lap. I ran my fingers gently through the fringes while he entertained me with his enthralling up close and personal stories about himself.

Kenny just kept talking about this and that but I could not concentrate on what he was saying to me because I was too busy concocting a plan to get laid.

"Are you putting me out Kenny?" I asked, in a somewhat sad, but playful tone.

"Of course not. I wouldn't do a thing like that," he replied, dryly.

"Good, because I wasn't ready to go yet," I said, bluntly.

"Well, I can hang for a while longer," said Kenny, coughing.

"How can I repay you for such a wonderful dinner? Would you like a neck massage?" I asked, hoping he would be agreeable.

I wanted to touch him so badly. I know it was an aggressive tactic, but I needed to get this party started somehow.

"Well... no that's okay Reina. Just sit here and relax. I don't want you to do any work. Tonight is all about you."

"That's really sweet of you Kenny. Do you always put other people before you, or is this a special occasion or something?" I asked, chuckling.

"I guess you could say that I'm pretty much the same way all of the time. I'd like to think that I'm a thoughtful man."

"You are very thoughtful. I'm having a fantastic time. Your home is extremely cozy and you are an incredible host."

"I'm glad you're having fun Reina. That makes me feel good."

I did not get a response from my first attempt at grabbing his attention, so I would have to go to plan B. I would try being more assertive this time.

"Oh, I'm having a ball," I said, as I reached over to hug him.

"The baby needed a hug?" he asked, in baby lingo as he hugged me back.

I made sure that the five-second embrace was as memorable to Kenny as it was for me. I hugged him with my face turned away from him at first; so that he could bask in the aroma of my freshly shampooed hair, then I turned back and ever so soothingly placed my parted lips on the meaty part of his neck so that he could feel the warmth from my face. As I released him, I confidently puckered my mouth and said, "Nice cologne" giving him a whiff of my fresh breath, compliments of the Altoid Company.

"Thank you," he smiled.

Mission accomplished...I think. He seems to have loosened up a little bit. I can sense that we were finally able to break the ice completely. Even though I felt comfortable in his presence, there was still something missing. I could not quite put my finger on it, but I feel a breath of fresh air blowing through the room.

"You're welcome."

The room was silent for a few moments. Neither one of us knew what the other would do next, so I took the lead. I wanted to know where his head was, so I would gave him a complement and he should in turn give me one right back. That's just the way it works. I was curious to know what he thought of the closeness we just encountered. Whatever his complement directs toward, will mean that was what he got most out of the hug.

"Wow! You have strong arms Kenny," I told him in order to get a response.

"And you smell great," he said, with his eyebrows raised.

I knew right then that he has a weakness for a good smelling woman. I would be at Saks first thing in the morning.

"Why thank you," I said, as I smiled on the inside.

"No, thank you."

"For what?" I asked, playing my dumb blond role.

"Uh, for gracing me with your sweet aroma?" he teased.

"Well I love to bathe with all kinds of body washes and I can't leave out of the house without dabbing a hint of perfume. I think I'm addicted to Victoria's secret."

"There's nothing wrong with that baby and it shows by how well you take care of yourself. I like that."

I scooted in even closer to him and put my head on his chest. I wanted to feel his heart beating. I could tell that he worked out a lot based on how cut and toned his body was. The more he resisted me the more turned on I became.

I couldn't take it anymore. My bosoms were silently crying out for him to touch them. I had to know how his lips tasted. I reached over to him and put my lips as close to his without touching them, because technically I wanted him to be the one to have kissed me first, so I didn't seem desperate, even to myself.

Kenny pecked my lips very gently one time when he realized how adamant I was, but I wanted more, so I stayed put in that exact position hoping he would peck them again.

I needed love at that very moment. Maybe he was just a bit shy so I was going in for the kill. I put my lips on his and began kissing him gently. He seemed to share in my passion but I sensed a little bit of hesitation on his part.

"What's wrong baby?" I asked.

"I just think that we should take our time and get to know one another a little better before we...you know."

"Before we what, fool around?"

"Well, yeah. I guess that's what I'm saying."

"So are you saying that you don't want to kiss me?"

"No, I'm not saying that."

"Then what is it Kenny?"

"I just think that we should take it slowly, that's all."

"Okay that's fine. But tell me what you're really thinking? Where is this coming from?"

"I just don't want to rush things. I want to treat you with respect. I want to make sure that there won't be any regrets in the morning."

"Well that's very considerate of you to think of me in that way, but I'm okay with it. We can be intimate. I'm sure of what I want."

"You are making me feel like a piece of meat here, Reina."

"Are you kidding me?"

"Actually... no I'm very serious."

"Most men would be thrilled to jump my bones. What's wrong with you?"

"I just want to be committed to someone before I sleep with them. No more, no less."

"Wow Kenny. Are you serious?"

"Why is this so hard for you to believe Reina?"

"Well I guess I thought I was irresistible, but you are making me second guess myself."

"You are irresistible baby. I'm just tired of wham bammin a different person every night. I've been there and done that and believe me Reina, nothing good will come out of it."

Kenny got self-righteous on me. I could not believe what I was hearing. Was he turning me down? I don't think that had ever happened to me before, not me! I better go into the bathroom and double check myself. Maybe I had an unsightly booger hanging out of my nose and he was just too polite to tell me or there could be some colorful remnants of my dinner in between my teeth. Even if that were the case, he should still be able to overlook those little minute imperfections and feel taken aback by my beauty.

"I don't want you to wham bam me. Well...let me rephrase that. I do, but we don't have to wham bam tonight. We can just get close and cuddle for a while. But at some point, a good wham bam might be just what I need," I said, chuckling.

"Reina you are something else."

"So I've been told."

"Should I be scared?"

"Probably,"

We laughed a little more as Kenny held me in his arms close to him on the sofa. I did not want to wear out my welcome for the second time, so I offered to leave, hoping he would ask me to stay the night, better yet... move in, but no such luck. I gathered my things, pecked him on his lips, and then exited.

I hopped in my car and immediately looked at my cell phone to see if I had any missed calls. I had three. Kayla called once and Lance called twice. I listened to my voice mails to see how worried I should be before I get home, since it was almost midnight. He just called to say that he was over at his boy Tony's house watching the fight on pay per view.

My mind consumed with thoughts of Kenny the whole ride home. Now, I had to go and see what kind of mood Lance was in. I hoped he didn't want to have sex tonight, since it had been two weeks since our last rumble in the hay. I was hoping I would be rumbling in the hay with Kenny right then. I was aroused just at the thought of him. I don't know what to do. Well... yes I do. I have a fantastic idea. I pulled up into my driveway and dashed into the house as quickly as I could so that I could go upstairs; lock my bedroom door in case Lance came home before I finished making love to Kenny. I went into my drawer, got my silver bullet that I purchased at a fun party, and then climbed into bed. I turned on my stomach and put my hands in between my thighs. My body grooved to its own rhythm. I wanted so desperately for Kenny to come and plug me up with his love. I slid a pillow under my bottom half, tooted myself up, and pretended he crept up behind me under the comforter, inserting me from the back. My womanhood throbbed extremely hard, as I touched it in a way that no one else could, except me. I softly called out his name. "Oooh Kenny." I gently kissed the sheets, as if it were his lips and got an unbelievable sensation. My body painfully ached for his erection. I felt like I was going to explode. Kenny did things to me that he knew nothing about. Whew! I have taken the art of loving myself to a completely new level. I didn't know what I was going to do about Lance now that Kenny and I had consummated our relationship. I guess I better get up and unlock the door. God, I hope I am fast asleep by the time Lance gets home.

# Chapter 11

The sun peeked in at me through my canary colored draperies as I tried to get the last few minutes of sleep in before heading to work. I had taken quite a bit of time off because I felt the urge to play hooky. My trip to New York did me some good. Seeing my friend Gina again was great. I needed to get away from the realities of my day-to-day life. Then going on a date with Kenny to his covert love nest was the icing on the cake. Now playtime must end. Well, for now anyway.

When my mind landed on Kenny, I jumped out of bed with a smile on my face that just would not quit. I felt like I just had the best sex of my life last night, although Kenny never laid a fingernail on me, well... not directly anyway. I felt energized and ready to face life head on.

I really enjoyed my date with Kenny, even though he was playing hard to get. I thought it was rather cute, actually. The more I thought about it, the more I liked the challenge. Guys are too easy these days. Most of them will consider a rendezvous with you as long as you are cute, and don't talk about if you have a size D cup bra and a big booty.

Kenny taught me something. I thought I knew everything there was to know about the male species, but there are still some descent men out there, judging from my date last night. For a man to be able to resist me was admirable, especially if they were not involved with anyone, because I knew I was irresistible.

Growing up, I didn't have much self-esteem. I was a late bloomer. I did not receive my greatest assets as early as all of my other class-mates, but as soon as I hit twenty-one I blossomed out of control and now I can't walk from my car into the grocery store without being hooted and hollered at.

Lance came home shortly after I unlocked the bedroom door last night. That was truly, what you would call perfect timing. I pretended to have been asleep for hours, though. He never knew the difference. I was prepared, in case he decided to ask me why I did not stay at Kayla's house, as planned; I would just say that she and her boyfriend Luther got into a big fight, so I left.

I walked over to my vanity and pulled open the bottom drawer, which housed my intimate toy collection, a few lingerie items, and my diary. I couldn't let another minute go by without writing down my most personal and private thoughts about the night before that were only between me, myself and I. Lance tried to obtain the contents of the diary once before, that I know of. I realized it one day when I went to write in it. I noticed that the lock had little scratches on it. It looked as if he put an Allen wrench in the hole and dug. Did he think I would not notice the scratches? I know he had to be disappointed that his attempt at breaking and entering was unsuccessful. He never mentioned it to me and I never mentioned it to him. It was no need for me to make him look like a complete idiot by asking him if he was the culprit, because I already knew what happened to it, duh! I don't think a robber broke into our condo only to read my diary and not ...rob us. I wasn't surprised at all. Lance could be sneaky at times, but it wasn't necessary to call him out on the matter. I would just use the information to my advantage for future reference.

I marveled at the idea of pretending to be single. That way I didn't have to look over my shoulder or feel guilty when I had intimate thoughts of Kenny.

As I jotted down all of the juicy details that inhabited my mind about my date with Kenny, I felt consumed with pleasurable feelings.

One part of me was a bit nervous about publicizing my feelings in my diary though, in case Lance was ever victorious at getting the darn thing open. The other side of me didn't care if he found out what I had written. That was just how over with the relationship I was.

I felt compelled to call Kenny and tell him what a wonderful time I had with him. I picked up the cordless phone in the bedroom and dialed his number, which I had memorized. His phone never rang but I heard a voice on the other line saying, "hello."

"Hey you," I said, assuming it was Kenny since it was his number that I had dialed.

"Hey babe," said Lance.

"Lance?" I asked.

"Yeah, who did you think it was?"

"Uh ... What do you mean, who did I think it was? I know your voice, Lance." I trembled.

"Well, why did you...., anyway, I called because I charged two tickets to my credit card for us to see the Phantom of the Opera tonight. I know how you love that show. We've been fussing and fighting for awhile now and I'm willing to call a truce and put an end to it all. So how about it beautiful, will you be my date?"

"I'm really tired Lance. I don't feel so well."

"Oh, what's the matter, Babe?"

"Uh.... My sinuses are acting up."

"I'm sorry to hear that. Do you want me to come home and fix you some soup or something?"

"No thanks. I really don't think soup is going to help."

"Oh, ok then. How about I just come home and rub your feet?"

"Lance, don't make a big fuss! I'll be alright. I'll just pick up some medicine on my way to work."

"So you're going in today?"

"Yes. I've prolonged the inevitable for long enough."

"Well I have my cell in case you need me."

"Alright, thanks."

"Bye Babe."

"Bye."

That was so close. How in the world did Lance end up on the other line when I was trying to reach Kenny? He must have been calling me at the exact same time that I called Kenny. They say what's done in the dark will eventually come to the light, but damn, it had only been a day since my indiscretion, if you can even call it that. That seems a little quick to be coming to the light, if you ask me.

I couldn't lie: I was shaken up by that mishap. Was God trying to tell me something? I was too scared to call Kenny now. It almost seemed something out there in the universe, didn't not want me to contact him. Like gravity was pulling at my coattail. That was so bizarre.

I called in to my job, letting them know I was on my way. I hope I would be able to function efficiently once I got there. I felt so preoccupied and anxious. I didn't know what was wrong with me, but I knew I better not let it affect my job performance because if I remember correctly, Kenny did not offer to take care of me, as of yet. My ears were opened wide listening for him to say something of the sort and I am positive that I did not hear anything like that, so for now it seems, I'm on my own. Ms. Charlene was cool though, so the one thing that I was not worried about was job security. I would get there when I got there. I would just call Kenny from work. I needed to talk to him. I yearned to hear his voice that always pleasantly stroked me in a way that sent chills up my spine.

I entered my workplace and spotted a few pieces of furniture that were just sitting there waiting for me to upholster. I said my hellos to everyone who made comments like "hey there stranger." It did not bother me that my co-workers made fun of me because I knew they were all crazy about me. We just like to play and poke fun at each other.

I signed for a couple of small orders that had come in and did a little bit of inventory at my desk in the cluttered back office. I could not get my mind off Kenny and what a diamond in the rough he seemed to be. Whenever I had a thought of him, my body would quiver with excitement. I was just so glad that I didn't wear any tight jeans. After last night, I knew the slightest graze against myself would get me going all over again. That man had a certain affect on me. It was inexplicable.

While staring down at the chaotic mess of Styrofoam peanuts that had fallen from the boxes, with the box cutter in my right hand, my mind kept drifting on my new romance. I decided once again to just go ahead and give him another call. I hoped that nothing would go wrong this time.

"Hello," answered Kenny.

"Kenny Hey, How are you?" I asked, not telling him who I was, but hoping he already knew.

"Reina, what a nice surprise to hear from you, what's up?"

"Thank you Kenny. I just wanted to call to say again what a lovely time I had at your home yesterday evening."

"Oh. I'm glad you had a nice time. I have to say, I enjoyed your company as well, my sister."

"Would you like to do it again sometime?"

"Let me see how my week is going and I'll get back to you on that. Maybe next time we can have dinner at your place. I would love to see it. A person's home can tell you a lot about them, you know?"

Oh, boy here goes nothing. I need to think of a good lie quickly. I did not want him to know about Lance just yet. Coming to my house was obviously out of the question. How do I get out of this one? Should I tell him that I am having my house fumigated for termites this week? How about I'm having my parents fly in from Memphis to stay the weekend and it would not be appropriate to have company over while they're in town, especially in front of my dad. No matter how old I get, I will always be daddy's little girl... right? I got it! I will just say... no! I am Reina Ann Joseph. I don't have to explain a damn thing to anybody.

"Well Kenny, I can't have company at my house right now. My Goddaughter is temporarily staying with me. She is my best friend from high school's daughter and unfortunately, my friend has some serious issues. She's a drug addict, so I am doing what a good God-mother should do. I took her in. She was fifteen and very impression-able. I'm her only real role model right now. Her dad's in jail and her uncle molested her. She does not trust men, so I don't bring dates to the house, although she is starting to be interested in boys. I hope she does not turn out to be fast because of what she's been through. So,

I'm just keeping a real close eye on her," I said, with a straight face, but a terribly guilty conscience.

I guess I am not such a hard ass after all. I was sure that I was just going to say no to him, but I couldn't. I couldn't believe how quickly I was able to think of that lie. It just rolled off my tongue as if it were true. It was almost as if I believed it myself. That's scary. I hate lying, but I feel like I don't have much of a choice in the matter. I need to keep Lance until I find his replacement. Kenny sure seemed to be a good candidate, but it was still too soon to tell. I couldn't believe the predicament that I was about to get myself into. I could feel it. I hoped this would not turn out bad. I was so certain that Lance was such a pushover, until he glared at me with that crazed look in his eye for talking about his mama. I was not so sure anymore, after that. Sometimes I know I need a swift kick in the butt, to keep me focused. I did not want an abusive man beating me black and blue; however, I need a guy who won't allow me to push him around, either. I want a strong, yet sensitive man, who silently hears me when I speak to him without actually having to speak. Oh well, back to reality, earth to Reina. Who am I kidding? Was there anybody out there like that, maybe? I thought about taking out a personal ad once, but I didn't do it because I was afraid that it would make me look desperate. I have an image to uphold. I can't act like common folk. My friends and family have always put me on a pedestal. I must maintain that image. Sometimes it's hard, but I'm accustomed to it now.

"Oh Reina, what a noble act of kindness and generosity on your part, to give so much of yourself like that, makes me see you in a completely new light. I love it when our brothers and sisters can work with each other and stick together... like so many other cultures do. Look at those Asians. They all pile up in one house, share a vehicle, open up a store or something, and pool their resources together until they can branch out. They don't mind sharing with each other, unity! That's what I'm talking about," Kenny exclaimed, in his power to the people speech.

I was getting myself in deeper, every time I open my mouth. I was feeling excessively uncomfortable about lying to him like that. What if we start to really love each other and he found out that this so-called benevolent act of kindness, as he refers to it, was all just a cunning maneuver to gain his affections? Now I was going to have to buy a journal to write down all of the lies and deceptions that I was probably going to end up telling this man, just to be able to refer back to them later, if necessary.

"It's not that big of a deal Kenny, really."

"Sure it is Reina. It's such a common thing amongst us as a people to take advantage of each other that we truly think it's a normal way of life, but it shouldn't be."

"What do you mean?"

"Well, you know how we do it Reina. We will go into the white man's store and pay the asking price for anything and not say a thing about it...until we get outside to our cars and gripe about it to our significant others, but when we patronize our brother's little mom and pop shop we want to negotiate and haggle over the prices. I've even seen some people offer to barter somehow. I know a brother who is a painter by day, a disc jockey by night and an exotic dancer for private parties on the weekend. This brother has two jobs and a hustle on the side. Everything he buys he figures out a way to exchange services. It was serious to him though. He has six kids for six different women. He has perfected the art of bartering and has made it his fourth career. Now don't get me wrong. There's nothing wrong with bargaining, but why exclusively to our brothers and sisters establishments? Why don't we feel comfortable going into the white man's store with that same mentality? I'll tell you why, because over time the media and society has brainwashed us into thinking that we are inferior to the white man and are not worth as much as him, but don't believe the hype. I can read and write just like him, I have a college degree just like him and I can run just as fast as he runs, if not faster. I can play better sports than him and take his woman from him if I really wanted to, so if anybody should be intimidated, it sure isn't going to be me. But I just have to be real. If we could just stick together as a people, we would be off the chain sister, and I mean that literally. It's all about that unity we mentioned earlier. Many other races stick together as a family unit, but not us. We are in it for ourselves and it's just sad. We want to fight each other every chance we get, over a woman…or man. You know how we are? Furthermore, don't talk about our youth fighting over having better rims on his ride than the next brother. Why can't we go out there and work for what we want, just like our parents' generation did? They didn't have a lot of money, but it was honest work. Why get jealous and try to take what our brother has? As long as we continue to think like that, we'll stay divided. It just breaks my heart. It's going to take us as a people to want to change our situation. One person can't do it by themselves, although it is a start. Believe me sister, I've tried. Sometimes I see how ignorant my people act and I just want to throw my hands in the air and give up, but I can't. The system is set up that way. Sometimes I feel like there's no hope, but I would be doing my people a grave injustice if I was to do that and I wouldn't be any better than them. So I do what I can, when I can."

Kenny was just going on and on about the woeful plight of the black man. All I wanted to do was talk about us, but he was making it rather difficult.

"I understand your point, Kenny."

"Sorry if I get wound up baby girl. That's just a touchy subject for me, for many reasons, you just don't know."

"I can see that you have very strong emotions, about a lot of things. I can just imagine that you would be equally as passionate about your woman, right?"

"No doubt about it. I always give all of me to whoever I'm with. That's just the way I am."

"Well that's good to know."

"Reina, I have another call coming in on the other line; I will have to talk to you later."

"Yeah, okay, later it is, then. Have a wonderful day Kenny."

"Same to you, bye,"

"Bye."

Kenny hung up so quickly, to catch the other call. She must've been important, whoever she was, for him to get off the phone with me to talk to her. I did not like that. I am starting to question Kenny's motive's a little bit. Maybe I ought to keep my options open.

I finished my work for the day and headed home. I pressed the number three on my speed dial to call Kayla. I wanted her to meet me at our after work spot for happy hour but she said that she and Luther were planning a romantic evening at home. She said they ordered Chinese and were getting ready to watch a bootleg copy of the movie "Friday" that he made her watch at least once a month. That was Luther's all time favorite movie since he feels like he relates so closely with Chris Tucker's character. They both smoke weed every day; I don't know what she sees in that man. I couldn't do it. He was always between jobs and he went from one crisis to the next. If he didn't have Kayla and her uptown lap of luxury to bail him out of his life circumstances each time he got caught up doing something stupid, I don't know where he would be...come to think of it, yes I do...Angola prison, his second home.

When I finally made it home, I sat down on the sofa to relax for a while before I had to get up, wash a load of laundry, and cook dinner. I felt like being nice to Lance since Kenny ticked me off by taking that phone call.

I was in the kitchen, by the cooking alcove, de-veining the shrimp. I reached over to grab the bowl of fresh green beans from the marbled island and began snapping them when Lance walked through the door. I could hardly believe it. He was never home this early. He must be up to something. I hated that I was always suspicious of him lately, but I was. I finished cooking and we sat down to eat. I grabbed a bottle from the wine chiller and sat it flush with the two centerpiece vases. To complete my desired look of ambiance, I turned the round knob to dim the halogen lights that sat in the decorative pendants, which made it the perfect atmosphere for a romantic dinner. For some reason, Lance just kept on harping about going out tonight. He wanted to go to a club in the Warehouse District. Apparently, there was a special event featuring local writers and poets. He wanted to be there to hear one of his old friends from high school speak the spoken word. I could not get out of going, because he was so adamant. I got dressed and went along with his plans, to keep the peace. I could not legitimately get out of going anyway, since it was Friday and neither of us had to work the following day.

We arrived just in time to hear the charismatic Dr. William McHale speak in his baritone voice to the intent listeners about a very passionate piece he called *The Stone*. He blew us away, with his eloquent style of poetic lyrics that just glided off his tongue, as he breathed his convictions into the atmosphere. The poem was abstract yet simplistic. The air was as still as a picture and it was as quiet as a mouse, as he concluded his fluent verses, the crowd, enthralled by his words. All eyes were on him, including mine. I was afraid to blink for fear I may miss a millimeter of a second of his performance that had me more and more enchanted as each minute rolled by. I looked up at Lance and even he was motionlessly in awe.

After the show, we met up with William to congratulate him on his newly acquired PhD status and to commend him on a poem well conveyed. I could not help but notice how articulately he expressed himself. In my opinion, he was well worthy his Doctorate of Psychology degree. I would lie on his sofa any day, just to hear him speak.

Lance held my hand while we all chatted. I happened to look over my right shoulder and spotted a tall, dark, and handsome man standing over by the wall, eyeballing me up and down. When he was able to catch my eye, he nodded his head at me. I turned away quickly, because I could not risk Lance noticing us checking each other out. When I felt comfortable enough to look over at him, he signaled me his phone number. I was able to get all except the last two digits. We had a whole conversation in sign language. He subtly beckoned me to meet him by the restrooms in the back. It took me a few minutes to get up the nerve while contemplating how I would go about this sloppy plan, so I just made a dash for it. I told Lance that I had to go to the ladies' room and for them both to excuse me, so they did.

As I walked past the far-reaching bar and approached the restroom, he was already standing there, waiting on me. He cautiously handed me a piece of paper behind his back that read: "Donovan's cell," along with the digits and then walked away. We did not say a single word to one another. I didn't even know what his voice sounded like. I have never behaved so desperately in my entire life and to receive a phone number from a guy on the back of a gas station receipt instead of a business card was definitely a first.

I hurriedly walked back over to where Lance and William stood to avoid Lance being suspicious of me. They wrapped up their conversation and then we headed home. I drove my car because I felt like listening to my rap CD. Lance didn't let me play it in his car because he thought it was too vulgar. He said Jesus blessed him with his sports car and he refused to disrespect the Lord by playing offensive rap lyrics in it.

As we travelled on I 10 back home, Lance asked me for a piece of gum. It was in my Doonie & Bourke bag that I had thrown on the back seat. Lance reached back there to get it and started unzipping the zipper. I snatched it from him because I didn't want him to see Donovan's phone number that I stashed in there. Lance asked me why I snatched my purse away from him. I said I only had one piece left and he could not have it. I did it playfully, so that I wouldn't arouse his suspicion. It worked. He shook his head, called me stingy, and then started a conversation about how good it was to see his old friend again.

As soon as we got home, I ran into our half bath downstairs. I acted as if I had to use it bad so that I could dispose of the number in private. I turned on the water in the sink and let it trickle softly. I wanted it to sound like I was urinating. I took the number out of my purse and memorized it, in a matter of seconds. I said it repeatedly to myself so that I would not forget it. I balled it up tightly, threw it in the toilet and then flushed, in case Lance walked by on his way into the kitchen for a late night snack. I stood over the toilet until the water stopped swirling around the bowl to ensure that the paper had positively gone down the drain and it had. I was free of all incriminating evidence.

I went upstairs, took a hot shower, wrapped my hair and then crawled into bed, as if nothing had happened. Lance wanted to make love. I told him that my menstrual cycle was coming soon and I had cramps, which it actually was, and I actually did. He left it at that; saved by the bell.

Lance woke me up the next morning with breakfast in bed. He sat the serving tray on the edge of my side of the bed, next to my silk scarf that had slipped off my head sometime during the night. He brought me eggs Benedict, hot tea and two Midol pills. He said the warmth of the tea would help to soothe my cramps, which it did. I nibbled on my food a little bit and managed to finish all of my tea. Afterwards, I decided to get up and go to the library to rent some books to read over the next few weeks. My girl Kayla told me about a good book called: *On the down low*. She told me all about it, but I wanted to read it for myself, especially since I sometimes visit the Atlanta area, where a lot of the low-down, I mean down-low men are.

As I got dressed, Lance asked me to go to church with him and his mother on Sunday. He said that he wanted us to start acting more like a family and he thought that it would allow for Ms. Pearl and me to get closer. Why does he all of a sudden want to be this Christian family man? What happened to hanging out with the fellas?

I agreed to go only because I had not been to church in a long while. I had grown up in the church so when I grew to be an adult I did not want to see the inside of one. My parents dragged me kicking and screaming` to worship service several times a week, either for choir rehearsal or for somebody's convocation, musical, revival, or anniversary celebration. And on New Year's Eve we had to spend the whole night praying and sleeping on the pews. All of my friends spent their Eve watching fireworks somewhere, partying and making out with their date for the night; all of the things that I wanted to do.

Instead, my folks forced me to sit in church with people three times my age singing those old church hymns. Every year I would come home with scuffed up knees from kneeling on those little cheap rugs all night.

While I was at the library, I decided to give Donovan a quick call. I dialed star-six-seven to block my number so that he could not call me back, but he did not answer. I left a short message telling him who I was and that I would try back at a later time. I was disappointed because I wanted to hear what his voice sounded like, but instead I met some woman's voice saying that Donovan was not available now. I doubt if it was his girlfriend since he gave me the number to call. I made sure I erased the number from my outgoing calls, incase Lance ever felt the need to go through my phone.

When I got home Lance was in the middle of the living room floor doing one arm pushups. I walked around him and plopped down on the couch with my three hard cover books that I had checked out from the library. I opened one of them and began reading the beginning of the introduction but Lance bouncing up and down with no shirt on at a count of almost a hundred kept distracting me. After he finished the ones on the floor, he flipped himself upside down; standing on his hands against the wall, doing additional fifty-jailhouse push-ups, as he called them. I didn't know how he knew what jailhouse push-ups were because he had never seen the inside of a jail. He had never been to visit anybody in jail, much less being in there himself. He was really a stand up kind of guy. He stayed far away from trouble. I don't think he has ever had a parking ticket in his whole life.

I was still very attracted to Lance, but it was just a little too late to mend all of my hurt feelings. I couldn't forget about all of the lonely nights I spent alone and all of the times he stood me up to take care of his family, as if their needs were more important than mine. The feeling of neglect was a hurtful thing and I refused to forget about it. Bringing me flowers and cooking me breakfast was just not enough to mend my broken heart. It used to be when I did not have any other options, but now I do.

It was Sunday morning, and the church filled quickly. We sat somewhere in the middle of the enormous congregation watching the service in person and on the big screen televisions. The sermon was about speaking life or death into existence with your words. It was a powerful message. It made me want to watch more carefully the words that come out of my mouth.

Ms. Pearl had the best time of all, dancing in the aisles. She even hugged me after service let out and invited us both over to her house for a home cooked dinner. Of course, that was Lance's Sunday tradition anyway, so we ended up over there, as I knew we would. After we ate, I offered to help with the dishes, even though I hate doing dishes. She declined my help and I was glad. She said nobody could clean her dishes or her house the way she liked it except her, so she would just rather do it herself. I don't see how she does it, all of those pots and pans and baking dishes. She didn't even have a dishwasher.

Lance and I headed back to our home in silence. Surprisingly, we were not at each other's throats, but instead, we just sat in the car mutually quiet, listening to the music and thinking on the day. I guess we both figured if we didn't talk to each other it would be more peaceful, something that we both craved. Neither one of us liked to argue. When we first got together and started dating, we never argued. We got along really well. We knew which buttons not to push and we did not push them, but then the respect level wasn't there as it was before so we ended up pushing the buttons like crazy, without a second thought.

Lance fell fast asleep on the living room couch. I headed upstairs to the bedroom and decided to call Donovan again. I was so curious about him. I wanted to speak to him to break the ice. Finally, he answered the phone and we made dinner arrangements.

I was having my monthly book club meeting at our condo the next evening. I needed to prepare the list of dishes I would have Maggie cook for my guests. It seemed like each of the members of the club had a different nutritional request. One did not eat pork, another dairy, and another was a strict vegan. Poor Maggie had the task of cooking a meal that would suit us all, which always ended up being a salad and fish of some sort.

The house was spotless. I was proud of the way my home looked when it had been spring-cleaned. When my house was disorderly, my brain felt cluttered, but when it was not, I could think clearly. I was ready to welcome my guests.

This was the first time in a long time that all ten members of the book club showed up. Denise, our treasurer, collected the dues as we all ate our salads and fresh fruit as appetizers. Some of the girls drank wine and the others opted for green tea. These were all professional women with very good jobs, who exercised regularly and ate properly but there was one thing that they all had in common, nobody had a man. Joyce and I were the only women in the bunch with husbands; the rest had the pleasure of living the single life, which all of them hated dearly. This was a classic case of the grass appearing greener on the other side. At book club meeting, we discussed the book of the month, but somewhere in the middle of the discussion, we always seemed to get side tracked, talking about real life man verses woman issues. If nothing else that subject alone could keep us talking into the wee hours of the night. I usually had to interrupt the discussion to tell them that we would reconvene next month, same time, and place. I loved hosting the meetings at my place. It gave me something to look forward to all month. Lance usually stayed out until he thought we were finished, because the one time he came home early, the girls attacked the male species and there weren't any other men there to back him up; so after that, he made sure that they were all gone before he came home. I couldn't say that I blame him, though.

# Chapter 12

I intentionally arrived at the dimly lit French Quarter restaurant fifteen minutes late. I had to make Donovan sweat a little bit. I did not want to seem too anxious. He stood up, greeted me with a bouquet of flowers, and even pushed in my chair. I was impressed, because after the way we met, I was sure that he would turn out to be a complete jerk, but I could not turn down a free meal. Unexpectedly, we had many things in common. We were both on the track team at our high schools and we had watched quite a few of the same movies. I could tell that he liked fashion as much as I did, maybe even more which was one of the things that drew me to him, in the first place. I love a man who has his own unique style and did not feel the need to follow all of the fashion trends of the season, like everyone else.

We talked about our short and long-term goals, where we saw ourselves down the road, although, I found it odd that he didn't ask about Lance, especially since he had seen us together. He ordered a couple of appetizers for us and a bottle of red wine. We nibbled and talked, talked and nibbled. The stuffed artichoke was divine. He made me laugh a lot which was a big part of the criteria for dating, in my opinion. We talked about how we could not pronounce half of the dishes on the menu. We looked all around the restaurant trying to figure out which men were there with their wives and which ones were there with their mistresses, just for fun, while waiting on our entrées. Donovan got a real kick out of it. Underneath the tablecloth, he slid his left hand on my cross-legged, smoothly shaven knee, smiling at me, as if he wanted my approval. I thought it was a bit soon for that, but I didn't say anything, because everything was going so great. I did not want to spoil the moment by being a prude, just because I found him to be a little presumptuous. He was right in the middle of feeding me a fork full of my tiramisu dessert when suddenly I heard "Who is this Bitch?" I turned around, to see this tall, belligerent female waltzing towards me, yelling and cursing profanities at us. Everyone stopped what they were doing to observe our table. We had become the spectacle of the moment, in a matter of seconds. I was mortified!

Another woman wearing the latest styled corn rolls in her hair, stood sturdily by her side, cracking her knuckles, as she spit out those venomous words. Meanwhile, she kicked off her untied Timberland boots and started taking off her gold hoop earrings and handing them over to her husky built comrade. I thought I was going to have to fight this irate woman, over a man I hardly knew. She asked me all kinds of questions, "how do I know her man," and "have we had sex?" I was in shock. I could not grasp what was happening, so I just sat there listening to her belt out those humiliating accusations, while Donovan's expression looked as if he had been sucking on a lemon.

"Whack," she smacked Donovan's face as hard as she could, while huffing and puffing. The manager and a high-strung security guard came running over to our table to silence the outrage, before it got more out of hand. The other patrons in the restaurant scooted in closer to each other, so they could discreetly murmur about us. I had never been so embarrassed in my entire life. Security escorted the two females out of the fine dining restaurant into the street, while kicking and screaming. Donovan made tracks outside behind them to console his live-in girlfriend, slash baby's mama of eight years. He tried to get back into her good graces, while I sat there at the table by myself taking in all of the stares.

I literally could not move. My body was numb from shock and embarrassment. It all happened so fast. I did not see it coming. I tried my best to get up, but my body refused. The exasperated manager ran back over to my table, panting, saying that I would have to pay the bill because the combative couple hopped in their cars and left. He overheard the female threatening to kill Donovan if he paid for the check. Not only was I ashamed that people were looking at me thinking that I dated married men, but appalled as well that Donovan would leave me stuck with the check, just because his baby's mama forbad him to pay.

I gave the manager my credit card. I waited mortified with my head in my lap until he brought it back to me. I found the strength from somewhere to get up and leave. I had hoped my legs would carry me all the way to the door without collapsing. I did not look anyone in the face as I walked by them on my way to the revolving glass doors, but I could feel judgmental eyeballs all over me. When I finally made it outside, I felt relieved of all of the stares, at least. I will never in life, step foot in that restaurant again, as long as I live and I am sure the management would appreciate that sentiment as well.

I drove all the way home in disbelief. When I got there, Lance was watching a football game and eating some spicy hot wings. I spoke to him and then made my way to our room where I could gather my thoughts in private. He was saying something to me, as I climbed the stairs but I was not coherent. I couldn't even walk straight; I kept wobbling, while grazing the wall on the way up. It was almost as if I were drunk. I only had one glass of wine.

I took two Tylenol pm to help me fall deep into a coma, but ended up waking up the next morning with a clear recollection of the previous night's fiasco.

I went in to work and tried to pretend that last night did not happen. I tried to manipulate my mind into thinking that it was all just a bad dream. It worked for a couple of days until Donovan called my cell phone to apologize and explain that the mysterious woman was his ex-girlfriend and how there was nothing between them. He said she must have found out the password and checked his phone messages. I just told him to lose my number. I could not fathom why he would even ask me to go out again, to make it up to me.

It took me almost a week to come down off that adrenaline rush. I didn't know what type of female she was, or if it was even over for her, so I went to the pawn shop and registered for a pistol, in case I ever got a knock on my door.

Lance would have a fit if he knew that I bought a gun. He does not approve of them. He said they are more trouble than they are worth.

Kayla met me at Café Du Monde for coffee and beignets after work, so she could hear all about the incident at the restaurant. As I was telling her the story, she just kept saying "What? Hell Naw... What?" She could not believe her ears. When I told her the part about him running out on the check, she cracked up laughing, saying, "That's so typical." I personally didn't see the humor in it, but she did.

There was a handsome fellow sitting a few tables away from us, wearing headphones and typing on his laptop. I noticed how he periodically looked over my way, but I did not pay him any attention. When we were getting up to leave, he got up also, and walked over to where we were. He took the liberty of joining us and then introduced himself as Mitch. I was apprehensive to converse with him because I didn't know what type of drama he would bring into my life. After Donovan, I was skeptical of meeting strange men. We all sat back down under the large awning and talked for a while longer. Kayla was impressed with the fact that he was the CEO of a music company. He gave us both very professional looking business cards on extremely expensive stock paper. She has always had a secret desire of being a professional singer, but never could get a break. He said that we could come by his studio sometime and check it out. He wanted me to see him in his element. Kayla was excited because she just knew that she was finally about to make her debut album.

As we all chatted Kayla received a call from Luther telling her to meet him at the Second line parade under the bridge on Claiborne Avenue. I was not ready to go home, so I tagged along with them. The Indians wore their colorful handcrafted signature outfits with the feathered hats and matching gear, marching up and down the streets to the sounds of their own chants. Luther twirled his umbrella, drunkenly skipped, and hopped to the beat of his own drum, as did many of the other participants.

Luther had carried on so, that he worked up a voracious appetite and had to buy a lucky dog from a red mobile stand rolling down the street, shaped like a big hot dog. Kayla and I walked behind Luther so that we could enjoy the entertainment he brought about. We followed him into a corner store so he could buy another forty-ounce beer to accompany him on the remainder of our one and a half mile walk. Luckily, I wore flip-flops and a tank top because it was scorching hot outside.

When I made it home, I noticed that I had tan lines on my shoulders from the straps. I rubbed some cocoa butter on my body and then relaxed on the sofa.

Kayla called me to say that she made it home. She worried me about calling Mitch for almost a week, but I just took my sweet time. I figured I was worth waiting for, and besides that, I had to do some investigative work. I went on the internet and googled him, then pulled up the Orleans Parish Probate Court and searched for his full name to see if he was married. I was surprised to see that his name was not on the list. Still, I did not want to rush into anything this time. I wanted to talk on the phone until I felt unquestionably comfortable with the fact that he for sure did not have a wife, girlfriend, live-in coochie or whatever. I wanted to see if there would be anything shady about him.

Since I couldn't find any dirt on Mitch, I decided to give him a call. I grabbed my cell phone and started pushing the buttons. I had saved his number under a different name, Michelle.

"Hello, may I speak to Mitch please."

This him, who dis?"

"This is Reina, from the coffee house."

"What coffee house?"

"Are you serious?"

"I'm jus sayin ma, I meet so many people due to my business, and it's hard to remember everybody I talk to."

"Uh huh, how about Café' Du Monde, does that ring a bell?"

"Ohhhh, now I know who you are. How you doin?"

"I'm fine," I responded coldly."

"Well what's up then, you wanna come by the studio for a minute?"

"I don't know now. You didn't even know who I was."

"I'm sorry sweetheart, let me make it up to you, come on over here."

"I'll think about it."

"Well I can't wait to see you, so hurry up."

"Hold your horses. I'll swing by for a little while on Saturday. Will you be there then?"

"I'm always here, ya heard me, see you then."

"Okay, bye."

We ended up going to the studio on Saturday morning, after I had left the gym. I was exhausted from my intense spinning class as well as doing cardio on the elliptical machine. I did not even take a shower. I had sweat spots under my arms and in between, my legs but I didn't care. I went straight there because I was not trying to impress this man. He should be trying to impress me. Maybe a part of me wanted to turn him off, as a protective mechanism so he couldn't hurt or disappoint me. Lance was out doing God knows what, so I had the day to myself and that was just lovely by me.

When we arrived, there were a couple of guys downstairs who greeted us by the freight elevators and escorted us up to the top floor where Mitch and the rest of the want to be rapper dudes were. They all seemed to cater to Mitch. Whatever he said went without question. He made one light skinned brother who was comfortably sitting with his feet propped up, eating a pig's lip get up out of a chair so that he could sit there, just by looking at him. Kayla thought she had died and gone to heaven. She always did love hanging with the fellas, as if she were one herself. Mitch told one of his boys to call and order food for everybody from a nearby restaurant. When Mitch spoke, everybody listened. He seemed to have power over them. I spotted a tattoo with a long stretched out word that read *boss man* sliding downward his arm. I liked watching him take control. Seeing him in charge like that and doing his thing made me feel important to be his date for the evening.

We listened to them put beats together on that gigantic switchboard with all of those hundreds of knobs, while eating our Chinese take-out that sat on a tall stack of Maxim magazines, improvising as a coffee table.

I got up to go to the bathroom. When I came out, there was a guy wearing sagging khaki dickies standing right outside of the door, with a chewed up toothpick hanging from his severely chapped lips, emptying all of the tobacco out of his cigar in to the waste basket. He was getting ready to roll a joint while waiting on me to come out, so that he could ask me if I would go in the back room with him to give him a lap dance. He apparently thought that Kayla and I were there to strip or turn tricks. I don't know what he thought, but I was pissed. I walked back over to the cigarette burned sofa where Kayla and I sat and whispered what the guy said to me, in her ear. She cringed and then turned around to look at him with raised eyebrows. He boldly beckoned her to go back there too. We were beside ourselves. I did not know if I should tell Mitch because he might not believe me if his boy denied it and I would look like a troublemaker, so Kayla and I decided to just be cool and let it slide, for now anyway.

Kayla convinced Mitch to let her sing in the soundproof booth, as Angela Bassett did in *What's Love got to do with it*. The fella's puffed, puffed, and then passed around a big blunt amongst them, as she crooned to herself, as if she were rehearsing before her big production on a stage in front of thousands of people. I watched her perform for us and chuckled to myself. I actually did not know that she could sing that well.

Kayla and I had a nice time at the studio. Mitch invited us to come again at some point, and we agreed. Kayla thought that I should give him a chance and not compare him to all of the other jerks that I have dated, but it was hard not to.

Mitch walked us down to our car himself, instead of one of his personal assistants and even displayed a hint of chivalry by opening my door for me. Before I could slide into my seat, he spun me around, threw me up against the car, pulled my hair, and stuck his tongue down my throat. His lips were very soft. I liked the way he took control of me. He was rough, yet passionate just as I liked it, but most importantly, he did not get slobber all over my face. I enjoyed the spontaneity of sucking face like they do on the soap operas in the moonlight, underneath the stars in front of an audience, well it was only Kayla there, but it was great nonetheless. I've always been a hopeless romantic.

The night ended on a good note, so I went home with the thoughts that I may try him and see what he was all about.

I didn't know what was happening, but it seemed like men were starting to come out of the woodwork all of a sudden. I guess it was true what they say, when it rains, it pours.

# Chapter 13

Mitch decided to woo me with his thug passion by setting up a nice picnic at Audubon Park. He brought along his laptop so that we could listen to music and a wicker basket full of ham sandwiches, some strawberries in a Ziploc bag and a bottle of Hennessey accompanied by red plastic cups. I had not been on a picnic, ever. I guess Lance and I just never got around to it. It was nice. We sat on his lint-ridden navy blue nylon blanket that has probably been to countless picnics, under a large oak tree, smooched for a while, and then decided to get up and take a stroll. He helped me up and then handed me my cup. We walked barefoot through the grass holding hands with our fingers interwoven as if we had been together for years. We were both well within our comfort zone, sharing stories about our past ex-loves. He made me feel so special but as I recalled, it's always good in the beginning of any courtship.

Mitch suggested that we top off our date by spending the rest of the day together. We went to a little night spot that he knew of in Algiers, not too far from the levee. On the ride there, he freaked a black and mild cigar to smoke on the way. I told him that I had never seen anybody do that before, so he pulled the car over and gave me a quick "How to freak a black lesson 101." We smoked it on the way to the bar. When we arrived, I got out of his fully loaded Lincoln Navigator and wiped all of the excess tobacco off my jeans.

I immediately went into the bathroom of the club to call Lance. Luckily, his voice mail picked up, so I just left a quick message saying that I was hanging out with Kayla. After I hung up with him, I called

Kayla to have her cover for me in case he called her for any reason. Lance has been known to do off beat things like that before.

Mitch seated us in a corner that we had all to ourselves. There were not very many patrons when we first arrived so it was nice not having to vie for the server's attention. The whole place, adorned with different colored light bulbs, to remind us of the nineteen seventy's era. It was so romantic. Each table had its own lit candle encased in glass on it. There were mirrors throughout the entire place. Mitch had his strapping arm around my neck and we sat back in our padded booth listening to Al Green, Marvin Gaye, Johnny Taylor, and Luther Vandross, while tapping our feet. Whoever played the last five songs had to be depressed because according to the lyrics "he was tired of being alone and needed some sexual healing after he spent his last two dollars on the jukebox because his house just ain't a home without his baby." After all of his selections were exhausted, I hurried to the jukebox myself and inserted two dollars for five songs before that guy tried to play some more of his gloomy tunes. I played songs relevant to my feelings about Mitch and me now.

I had not been to a hole in the wall bar like that since I used to go with my Uncle Sylvester back in the day in Woodville. The server came over to where we were sitting with her pen and notepad, to take our drink order. She and Mitch evidently knew each other because they hugged and started talking about things that were unknown to me. I did not feel like I was a part of the conversation, but I smiled anyway the whole time, just to be cordial. He was complementing her perfume and touching her arms and hands every time it was his turn to talk. I was starting to feel a little uncomfortable but I figured that I was overreacting, so I let it go.

Joan, our server, left to get our drinks and I was able to regain his attention. He started talking about how much he loved that club and the atmosphere. In walk, these two females and he stared at them until they took their seats. I was still talking to him and he would answer my questions and nod his head, still looking over at their table. I was not sure if he was being rude, or if he thought, he knew them, or what. I did not want to seem insecure by bringing it to his attention, so I did not say anything. I just kept talking, trying my best not to get upset.

One of the girls with a rather large behind got up to go to the restroom. Shortly after Mitch said, he had to go too. I thought that it was quite odd that he had to go at almost at the exact time as the female, but once again, I second-guessed myself thinking that maybe it was really just a coincidence. I noticed that the two of them had both been gone longer than need be so I did a little investigative work by walking over to the bar and positioning myself in a perfect place to see him talking to her in the back by the cigarette machine. They did not see me. I went back to our table where I was initially so happy and excited to be and now was not. I waited for him to come back, but the female walked out first, as if they had planned it that way to look as if they were not talking. If I had not used that same tactic myself back in the day maybe I would not have been suspicious, but I was and for good reason, it seemed.

Mitch returned shortly and I noticed that he did not snuggle up close to me as he was before he left, so I decided to play a game with him. I pushed up so close to him, I was almost sitting in his lap. Surprisingly, he didn't push me off, but still I was angry. I did not know what to think, but I know what I felt. Periodically I would look over at the female and she would be looking right at us, but then she would turn her head quickly as if she were not looking. I put the moves on him so thick. Mitch was wondering what had gotten in to me.

We sat there long enough to finish our drink when he suggested that we go somewhere a little more upbeat. I was still mad at him, but I agreed because I was curious as to what he had in mind.

Under the green canopy at the front entrance, a big, blue black, brawny security guard, wearing a t-shirt a few sizes too small that read "Security" in bold font, searched thoroughly all through my purse. He even unzipped the zippers and looked in the tiniest compartments. I felt like an Iraqi woman at the airport. He was breathing hard and grunting under his breath. I sure hoped he did not have to chase anybody out of the club because he had enough trouble breathing just standing in one spot without wheezing. Mitch and I both got frisked right before they looked directly at me and asked me for twenty dollars. I looked at Mitch as if he had better pay for it, since he had brought me here and he did. I wondered why they did not charge Mitch anything. As soon as we walked through the metal detector and got the okay to go in, a couple of half naked girls wearing g-strings and garter belts came up to the front booth asking for change for large dollar bills, saying that there were some big spenders in the VIP section.

I could not believe that Mitch had the audacity to bring me to a strip club, on our first date at that. Did I give off the impression that I wanted to watch women shake their asses tonight or at all for that matter? After the initial shock, I decided to be a good sport. After all, we did just spend fifteen minutes trying to get in the club; we may as well try to have a good time.

We sat at a small square shaped wooden table close to the bar, but not far from the stage. There were a few women sprinkled in the audience. I felt slightly embarrassed, as if I were there to check out the dancers. I was hoping I did not see anybody I knew. The chances were slim because Lance and his friends didn't like strip clubs.

A host wearing a pair of spinning pasties and a mini skirt so short we could see her butt cheeks came over to take our drink order. Mitch appeared to be in Heaven. He seemed to be struggling with having to juggle watching the naked girls walk back and forth and the girls on stage sliding up and down the pole. He put his large arm around me as we watched the show. I must admit, the longer we sat there, the more my attitude manifested.

An attractive light brown skin sister wearing a Halle Berry haircut and a smile walked up to our table and offered Mitch a lap dance. I expected him to decline, but he gladly accepted and handed her a crisp ten-dollar bill that he pulled from his money clip. The woman in the black sequined thong started moving to the music, putting her six-inch clear stilettos in between his legs to touch his crouch with the ball of her foot, while doing seductive flips across his lap. She took her shoes off, stood up backwards on both of his knees, and did a jig with her well-rounded booty in his face. It looked as if she did squats everyday to get booty like that. I tried not to stare at them while she danced for him, but out of the corner of my eye, I saw him rub both of his hands from the small of her back all the way down to the crease that separates her butt from her legs. I could feel myself getting more jealous by the minute, so I just sat there. The next thing I know she had performed a split on the floor that led her over to my chair. She did a handstand, flipped herself forward, and landed right in my lap. She caught me off guard. Mitch was having a ball. He smiled so big, I think I saw his tonsils.

When the song ended, she politely said, thank you and then immediately walked over to the next table where three single brothers in business suits were heckling, while waiting on their turn. I looked down at his lap to see if he had an erection and sure enough, there it was, standing as tall as Mount Everest. I felt so disrespected, all I wanted to do was go home and cry myself to sleep. My feelings were hurt, but I knew that I would not feel vindicated unless I avenged him. I felt uncontrollable angry emotions building into viciousness, so I fearlessly threw my half-full long island iced tea in his face and headed for the door. He dashed out behind me and yanked me back by my hair, asking me what my problem was. I turned around, started swinging my arms at him hoping to land a couple of licks right upside his head, without getting my ass beat down, but instead, I ended up barely scratching him on the side of his face with my fingernails. He unflinchingly grabbed me by both my arms to restrain me. Two big burly bouncers ran over to us, put Mitch in the figure-four chokehold, then bounced both of us right out of there, and ordered us not to return. I asked the bouncer if he would so kindly call a taxicab for me, so he did, just to get me out of there fast. Mitch stood there soaking wet, using his sleeve with the expensive cuff links on it to wipe his face.

Mitch called my cell phone for the extent of my whole ride home. I just let my voice mail pick up because I never wanted to see him again. I had absolutely nothing to say to him and I surely did not want to listen to anything that he had to tell me. I must have looked tousled because the taxi driver kept staring at me through the rear view mirror and asking me if I was okay. I paid my fare and then went inside. My phone was still vibrating so I turned the power completely off. When I woke up the next morning and listened to all seventeen of my missed calls from Mitch, I was frightened because he threatened to get his sisters and female cousins to whip my ass if he ever saw me out somewhere. He was the thug type in a business suit, so I knew not to underestimate him. Now I had to watch my back. I checked the times of all of his calls; his last one was at six o' clock in the morning.

I stayed in the house for three weeks straight, only going to work and back. Kayla was terribly disappointed that she did not get her record deal. I just kept thinking that if enough time were to pass, the less likely he would remember the incident or even care and the more at ease, I would feel.

Three weeks later, I opened the front door to pick up my paper to find a dozen dead roses lying on my welcome mat. I hurriedly closed the door because I did not know what to think. I had thoughts of Mitch running rapid all through my mind. How did he know where I lived? Was he after me? Should I call the police?

I didn't know what to do because I did not want Lance to know about this. I swept it under the rug while looking over my shoulder at every move I made. I felt so uneasy knowing this guy could show up at my front door anytime he felt like it.

I wrapped the flowers in the sports section of the newspaper, put it inside of a plastic grocery bag, and then walked it out to the dumpster. I looked to the left and the right of me, as I made my way to put out the trash. Each time a car passed me by, I stared in the window until I saw that it was not him.

Kayla's little brother Jeffrey was a police officer and he told me to let him know if anything out of the ordinary happened again, he would come right over to handle it.

I was too tired to dig into my lingerie drawer to get my journal last night, so I took a little time this morning to catch up on what happened on my date with Mitch.

I finally managed to get Kayla and Gina on three-way for the first time in a long time because one of us was always unavailable. We talked and talked about everything that had been going on in my life, like my job, my relationship and my upcoming family reunion. They were more interested in my life than talking about themselves.

They advised me to do so many things, so many ways that now my head was spinning. I probably should have just tried to work it out myself. I should have known better than to talk to the both of them at the same time, especially for hours at a time. I was more confused than I was before I called them.

I sat on the edge of the bed, feet dangling still in my matching two-piece camisole and panty set thinking about what I was going to do about Lance. I couldn't keep messing around behind his back, particularly with lunatics. I needed to formulate a plan and stick to it. I needed to compose a list of pros and cons to help me determine if I wanted to stay with him or not.

I pulled up a blank Word document and began typing my list on the laptop. Even though the pros list was longer than the con's, I still decided to give Kenny one more chance. We had not spoken in almost a month but I wanted to allow him the opportunity to prove himself worthy of me for the last time. I needed to know how he felt about me or if he could grow to feel the way that I wanted him to feel in the near future. I needed something to go on, so I called; this time from my cell phone.

"Kenny, heeyyyyy, its Reina,what's up?"

"Hey Ms. Reina, long time no hear baby girl."

"Yeah, everything's alright on my end, what about you, you been okay?"

"Just working like a Mexican is all."

"Have you thought about me? I haven't talked to you in weeks."

"Has it been that long?"

"Uh, yeah,"

"Of course I thought about you."

"Good, that's what I wanted to hear. It's time that we see each other again. What do you think?"

"Hmm, I'm tied up for the next couple of days, but after that I should be free."

"Well Kenny I guess we won't be able to do anything until next weekend then, because I just found out that we are having our family's reunion in Mississippi on Saturday. I really don't want to go, though."

"Why wouldn't you want to go to your family's reunion? That sounds like fun."

"Well let's just say that my family is a bit...dysfunctional. I guess that would be a good descriptive word."

"Whose family isn't? You better go to your reunion girl, eat that good barbeque, and meet your long lost cousins that you didn't know you had," Kenny teased.

"Yeah, they are badgering me, because I haven't gone for the past three years. So it looks like I can't skate out on them again this year."

"Well, just give me a buzz when you get back, if you like."

"Okay, I sure will. Talk to you later."

"Bye Reina."

I was truly hoping that Lance didn't want to go with me to Mississippi. He had never met any of my family before. I liked it like that. I was still not ready to show him where I grew up and better than that, how I grew up. We were extremely poor. I could remember when my adopted mother only allowed me to use two squares of toilet paper per time I urinated, to cut cost. I wore hand me down clothes and ate sandwiches for dinner many nights. What I did not understand was why my biological mother would give me up, because she had financial problems, just to give me to another family who had similar challenges? I have never been able to wrap my mind around that concept. My adopted mother said my biological mother was a drug addict and a prostitute. She claims she didn't know what ever happened to her and that it would cause too much heartache for me if I tried to find her. My family has many secrets and I just didn't need my Cousin Emma Jean getting all drunk, airing out all of our dirty laundry to Lance. That was the last thing I needed, Lance looking his nose down on me. I wanted him to go on thinking of me the way he thinks of me now, as the diva that I am. I couldn't afford to have his pure thoughts of me tainted.

# Chapter 14

"Babe, I'm so glad that this reunion came about when it did. You and I sure need this time alone together. Wouldn't you agree?"

"Sure," I said, looking out of the passenger side window with green bird poop on it, as Lance drove us across the Mississippi state line.

"Are you okay, you seem preoccupied babe?"

"Yeah, I'm fine."

"Well I know you really didn't want to come because you said that your family is down right crazy, but it'll be good for you to see all of them again. I even brought the digital camera so that we can laugh about it later. Don't worry Babe; I'll be right by your side."

Lance was trying to reassure me that things were going to be okay, when a big fat greasy faced truck driver cut us off and almost ran us off the highway, abruptly interrupting him. Lance got so upset; he gave the man his middle finger. The trucker in return gave Lance the bird right back and then they both cussed and fussed at each other, through the car's glass windows. I was frightened because the man in the truck looked as if he didn't have much to live for and would welcome a good old fashioned country brawl right there in the middle of the road. Lance honked his horn and the truck driver honked right back. The trucker's honk was much louder, though. I thought he was going to run us off the road, but instead he accelerated and took off fast.

"Lance, you could have killed us," I said, terrified.

"Awe he wasn't going to do anything."

"You don't know that for sure."

"Just forget about it Reina. It's over now."

I sat in my seat looking at Lance, listening to him talk about the incident, as if it was nothing. He didn't see that he put us in harm's way. I was appalled.

As soon as we pulled in to the elongated driveway, Aunt Betty spotted me. I guess those thick bi-focal glasses of hers really came in handy. She threw her spatula on the grill and came running down the rocky driveway, wiping her hands on her already stained barbequing apron, screaming my name to the top of her lungs in excitement. She drew the attention of damn near the entire family to us. They all stopped what they were doing and headed down the gravel toward our car. Everybody started yelling and blaring at us, as if they just spotted Will and Jada. Lance was startled, but managed to keep that nervous smile on his face the whole time.

We hugged and kissed everyone for what seemed like an eternity. They forced Lance and me to eat a big plate of food, declaring that we were both too skinny. We appeased all of the interested parties by telling stories about what I'd been up to since they'd seen me last. They bombarded Lance with all kinds of questions about himself, because they had never met him before.

Lance and I spent most of the day sitting in the front yard under my Aunt Betty's Pecan tree, talking with my over-enthusiastic Uncle Sylvester who had already drank himself into a stupor by the time we got there. He and Aunt Minnie had been married for about a lifetime but that didn't stop him from eyeballing everything walking around in a skirt, even if they were related to him. His famous motto of all time was "I ain't dead... yet."

"U sho is looking good there, Reina. I see you snagged yoself a redbone this time, huh?" said Unc, displaying his new denture set, with one lonely gold tooth on the top left.

"Yes. I did. This is my husband Lance," I blushed.

"Well howdy do there Lance?" he loudly blurted with a heavy southern drawl.

"How do you do, sir?"

"Oh, my ol stinky butt is alright, just tryin to make it, just tryin to make it."

"That's good to hear, sir."

"Why is your old butt stinky Unc?" I playfully yet hesitantly asked.

"Cause yo old ass Auntie don't wash my drawers when she get mad at me."

"Why is Auntie mad at you?"

"Cause she just downright evil!"

"Well I can't believe that about my Aunt Winnie."

"Well believe it! Her drawers is clean, but mines is dirty. I seen em for myself laying ner in the chifforobe, just as clean as they wanna be. She a evil witch I told you. She ain't even yo real Auntie anyway, ya know? She lucky I married her and let her come into this wonderful good-lookin family. Look atcha, looking so lovely. Turn around and let me take a good look atcha!"

"Well I'm sure that you guy's will work it out," I said, turning in a 360-degree circle.

"And she don't cook no mo neither."

"What? Why doesn't she cook?"

"Cause she tryin to starve me til I'm dead," Unc exclaimed, after taking a gulp of his beer.

"Oh Unc, don't say that. Aunt Winnie wouldn't do a thing like that."

"Why you think I'm so skinny? She starving me, I tell you. I don't get nuttna eat, lessen I come over Betty house fo a picnic or sumthn. If it wodn't fa my beer belly you wouldn't even see me sittin here. I'd been don disappeared by now."

Lance looked at me with a concerned expression on his face. Little did he know this was rather normal behavior coming from my family? I tried to warn him.

"So uh, Lawrence you must be takin real good care of this here gal, cause she sho is lookin especially good. Last time I seen you gal, you was a lil girl seem like?"

"Unc, his name is Lance and you can't flirt with me. I'm your niece."

"I know who you is. I ain't that drunk. I aint cha real Uncle anyway. You sho have some real perky titties there gal. I remember when yo lil titties used to look like dem raisins, you know da ones in da red box wit da lady holdin nem grapes," he went on, letting out a roaring burp.

"Unc, look at Aunt Winnie over there, she's a good looking woman, too."

"Yeah...she alright but her perky titty days is long gone. She saggin all over the place now. Why you think I like lookin at the young ladies? I ain't dead...yet."

"Unc," I said embarrassed.

"If God didn't intend for me to be lookin at titties he woulda made me blind long time ago."

"Okay Unc. It's no use is it?"

"Nope, don't think so."

Lance, appalled by the conversation with Uncle Sylvester, did not find a lick of humor in it at all. I guess I couldn't say that I blame him because Unc can be rather obnoxious, especially after a six-pack of his favorite malt liquor.

Uncle Sylvester sat sloppily in his lawn chair, wearing his barbeque rib stained family reunion t-shirt and his black church slacks pulled up to his shins to expose his thick white baseball socks with the blue stripes and black dress shoes. He sat accompanied by a two pack of beer, which initially started as a six-pack. He slurred out ridiculous story after story while rubbing on his wide beer belly the whole while.

Lance and I were so tired by night fall, we both just went into Aunt Betty's house where we were spending the night and prepared ourselves for a good night's rest. Lance was too tired to take a shower, collapsing across the foot of the bed, fully clothed. I went into the kitchen to have a cup of tea with a shot of honey with her before I turned in. The kitchen is where country folks like to engage company.

She always said that a hot toddy before bed would help to knock out a cold whether you had one or not.

Lance's sleep interrupted by the sound of my cell phone vibrating loudly through my purse. He tried to catch it in time to run and bring it to me because he knew that I had been expecting an important call from one of my sorority sisters about an upcoming convention.

He must have looked down at the phone, dashing out of the bedroom door and happened to notice that the screen said, Kenny, so he took the liberty of answering it. I don't know why I saved his number under his real name. I slipped that time. I was usually so good at covering my tracks. Lance walked in the kitchen with a sour look on his face, as he handed me the phone, already flipped outward. I saw that it was Kenny and started to talk to him as if he was one of my homeboys from way back. Lance stood in the same spot scrutinizing me and listening closely to my every word. I told Kenny that it was late and that I was tired so I would have to talk to him later.

When I got off the phone, Aunt Betty got up out of her chair with the flattened seat cushion and politely said that she was going to bed, but I knew that was just her way of giving us some privacy because it looked as if Lance was about to drop the clip and detonate any minute.

Lance interrogated me about the phone call about a half an hour, until his speech slurred from exhaustion. I just told him that Kenny was an old friend of mine from college that took a chance on calling me to see how I was doing, because we had not talked for a while. Luckily for me, I have had the same cell phone number for the past eight years to be able to use that as an excuse. Lance could hardly keep his eyes opened, so he instantaneously gave up, fell backwards onto a freshly washed fluffy pillow, and started snoring.

I was so happy that it worked out that way because I did not want to have a shouting match with him at my family's house. I set the alarm clock that sat on the scratched up wooden dresser on my side of the bed and tried to stay clear of Lance for the night.

First thing in the morning, we packed our bags, as per Lance's request and proceeded to head home, earlier than expected. Aunt

Betty had been up since dawn. She was in the kitchen boiling grits to go with the homemade pancakes and hot sausage patties that she had already cooked for us to eat, when we woke up. I thought it was very rude of us to leave so abruptly, but I knew that last night's phone call was still on Lance's mind, so I did not argue.

Since I didn't eat pork and the grits weren't ready, I put a single pancake on a paper plate and poured some of her homemade maple syrup to go and we bid her goodbye.

When Lance put the luggage in the trunk of the car, I noticed that he did not escort me to my side and open the door for me as he always did. He must've still been upset about that phone call, but he was being passive aggressive about it.

I gobbled up my perfectly round pancake so fast out of nervousness that I gave myself a terrible case of indigestion. I asked Lance to pull over into the nearest gas station. I wanted to purchase some chewable tablets.

When I returned, I observed that he had changed the compact disk from the nice rhythm and blues one that we were listening to; to a vulgar rap disc that he swore he would never play in his car. I knew then that something was wrong. I didn't know where he got it from but I knew it wasn't one of mine.

We rode silently, listening to the music, all the way home. I guess he thought he was punishing me by making me listen to the crude words that I'm sure he meant just for me, but little did he know, I tuned the words out and just paid strict attention to the beats. I love rap. I listened to it all the time when I drive, but I didn't play it around him, knowing how he felt about it.

When we finally arrived home, which seemed like an eternity, I hung my keys up on the key rack and headed upstairs to get ready for bed. I was mentally exhausted from quietly trying to pick Lance's brain all the way home. Even though we did not talk about it, it was heavily on my mind.

For the first time in a long time, we ended up going to bed at the same time. I would have loved to spoon him, but I knew that was not going to happen, so I lay on my back and stared at the ceiling for a while, until my eyes got heavy. He didn't say a single word to me which was surprising. Based on experiences in the past, he would have argued his point until the sun came up, but this time something was different. His demeanor was still and it became harder to read him.

# Chapter 15

When I pulled up in Kenny's driveway, I called his cell phone to let him know that I was outside. He came to the door looking even better that he did the first time I visited him. He just kept getting sexier and sexier every time I saw him.

Kenny was set on going out to eat at the Thai food Restaurant down the street from his house. He said we could actually walk there if we wanted to. It was a nice evening at dusk, not too warm or too cool, but just right. Even though I wanted to stay in for dinner, I agreed to go because I am a sucker for dining out.

We sat on pillows on the hardwood floor at a small round table, took our shoes off like all of the other patrons, and waited for our server. She came over carrying menus and a metal bowl with hot water in it and handed us both a warm washcloth that she rang out for us to cleanse our hands.

We ate our chicken and rice dishes with chopsticks. It was interesting watching Kenny twirl his around like a pair of numb chucks. I could tell that he had used them often. I tried not to make a fool of myself, so I told him that he would have to show me how to eat with them. He smiled, pulled my wooden sticks apart, and then educated me.

We took small footsteps for five short blocks back to his house As soon as he sat down on the couch; he picked up the remote and turned the television on. I jumped in his lap, straddling him. I stuck my tongue in his mouth, kissing him passionately. I wrapped both my arms tightly around his neck, as if I was holding on for dear life. He wrapped his muscular arms around my waist and that was when I let my body go limp within his affection.

I didn't feel anything poking me at first, but the longer I held on to him, the bigger he grew. I felt a thick, large piece of flesh rising in his pants, pressing against me. I did not move and his love muscle met me at my special place. I wanted him to enter with a sense of urgency. I was so aroused, I couldn't help it. I raised my skirt and began slowly grinding up and down on it, with every stroke; I pressed myself harder and harder against his love tissue hoping he would enter me. It was almost as if I were possessed. I could not diminish that feeling of ecstasy if I wanted to. I was in too deep. I imagined what it looked like in my head, as I dry humped him like a dog in heat. I pictured it to have long winding veins running throughout it. I could feel it thumping against me like the lead drummer at the battle of the bands during halftime at the Bayou Classic. My eyes were wide and intense, as he held me tighter with every thrust. I was throbbing and aching in places that have been asleep for a while. My body was stimulated into orbit without me removing a stitch of clothing. I released my sweet juices right into my panties.

Kenny said he would go downstairs to get a couple of towels out of the dryer, so I could clean myself off.

While he was gone, I was on my way to the bathroom when I passed his bedroom and saw his desktop modem was on. I was curious to see what his screen saver looked like. I barely touched the mouse and there was his "my space" page. I couldn't help but take a quick glance at his profile, because I didn't know he had one. It was set up nicely but I thought it was bizarre that all of his top friends were half naked men with names like "*Mandingo Warrior*" and "*Man 4 Man.*" I got down to the comments part of the page and saw remarks from men saying how much they enjoyed their conversations with him and asking when can they see him again. One guy wearing a jock strap, by the name of "*Strictly Dickly*" commented, "Same time, same place next week and you know where that is, lol?"

Something explicit caught my eye, so I clicked on Mandingo Warrior's page first, to find him standing there posing for the cameras in nothing but a miniature towel wrapped around his waist with a very visible erection peaking out. I scrolled down even further, trying to make sense of it as much as I could without getting caught red handed. I went into his inbox folder and read a few messages that he and Strictly Dickly sent back and forth to each other. I was horrified at what I read. Strictly Dickly expressed his gratitude for the erotic evening they shared, while recapping play by play graphic details in third person, as if he were role playing.

I heard footsteps coming back up the stairs, but there was so much more I wanted to investigate and not enough time. I second-guessed myself. I wondered if I read it wrong. Kenny couldn't be gay, he was not feminine at all and I did not know what to think.

I started to run out of his bedroom and pretend like I had not seen a thing, but I knew that I would not be able to contain that sickened feeling that had come over me for long, especially once my imagination started running completely wild.

"Reina, what are you doing in here?"

"Looking at your myspace page."

The room got silent. I stood looking at him up and down trying to find some clue about him that would give away his little dirty secret. I observed his mannerisms, the way he walked, talked, stood, and dressed... everything.

"Kenny, why do you have all of these naked men on your page?"

"Because, they're my friends,"

"Friends, what kind of friends?"

"Just friends, some with benefits,"

"Do you sleep with them?"

"Not all of them."

"Excuse me?"

"Only when I want some money,"

"What the hell?"

"What? What's the problem?" he said, nonchalantly, shrugging his shoulders.

"The problem is you're gay."

"First of all, I'm not gay, it's just sex. I don't go out looking for men like you think."

"What?"

"It's not a big deal Reina. What is your problem? A lot of straight guys are doing it."

"You are so gay. You were going to be my future man, that's my problem."

"I was?"

"So what are you telling me exactly, Kenny?"

"I'm glad you know about this now. It feels like a load has been lifted. I was going to tell you, but I didn't know how you would react."

"How did you think I would react?"

"Sort of like you are reacting now,"

"Smart ass, why did you kiss me and get intimate with me?"

"Because, I think you're cool and I'm attracted to you."

"That's it, I'm cool? I was going to leave my husband for you and all you can say is, I'm cool?"

"Your husband, I see I wasn't the only one hiding something?"

"Don't even try it. You know damn well that me being married doesn't even compare to you being gay."

"For the last time Reina, I'm not gay. We both held something back though. There's really no difference."

"Kenny, you poke dudes in the butt hole, that's disgusting... or do they poke you?"

"I'm always on top baby girl, could never be a bottom, okay?"

"Stop calling me that! I can't believe you're telling me this."

"Well if you don't feel comfortable talking about it, that's cool with me."

"Well of course I want to talk about it. I want to know what I've gotten myself into. Do I need to go to the clinic to get tested for anything?"

"Well, uhm...not really,"

"Well what?"

"Okay Reina, I will level with you, I found out that I was HIV positive quite some time ago, but we didn't do anything remember? You dry humped me."

"Oh My God; Oh My God; Oh My God,"

"Reina, you are fine, trust me. Why do you think I didn't touch you all of those times you threw yourself at me? I was protecting you."

"You let me kiss you Kenny. What about the kiss, our saliva?"

"You're fine; I didn't give you that much tongue, anyway."

"You should have told me, you asshole."

I cried because I did not know if I had just contracted a fatal disease from him. I didn't know enough about the subject to know how to feel about what had just happened. I put my hands over my entire face and slid down the bedroom wall that had been holding me up.

"I swear, I was going to tell you about my pastime, but I never felt like the time was right. I honestly didn't think you would understand."

"Understand, who in the hell would understand something like that?"

"The last girl I was with didn't have a problem with it. She liked girls on the side too."

"So let me get this straight. You sleep with men, or men and women, what?" I screamed.

"Reina calm down! I'm trying to be open with you here. I have a friend, but he's always touring with his band. I don't see him much though. I am mostly attracted to women, but I have been known to stray to the other side here and there. I got to get my hustle on, baby girl. That does not make me gay though."

"What do you think being gay is, you idiot?"

"I only do it when I need some quick cash. Obviously I like women, I was married wasn't I?"

"Well what about this friend that you were telling me about, are you just hustling him too?"

"Of course, but he knows what's up. He's a big time musician and he spends all of his money on me. A lot of guys like that have hustlers to bang them when they need it and in return I get paid. In this case, I just happened to hit the jackpot. He pays all my bills. I get front row seats, back stage passes, and limousine rides to any concert in the world."

"And what does he get in return?"

"Whatever he wants, I'm a hustler baby girl, and the bills have to get paid."

"Why don't you pay your own damn bills? You do work don't you?"

"I work, just not a nine to five gig, that's all,"

"I thought you went to college, got your degree, and worked doing some kind of African study thing. What the hell do you do then?"

"I told you how corporate America is and that's why I stepped away from it. I hang dry wall sometimes for a buddy of mine, when he has extra work."

"What?"

"I don't even have to do that because I'm well taken care of. I just do it to stay busy. Honest work never hurt anybody."

"Drywall, you're kidding me right?"

"What's wrong with that?"

"Nothing, I guess, but I just assumed...."

"Well, you assumed wrong."

"That's why you were covered in dust when I first met you, huh?"

"Yeah, I was working on a house in Marrero."

"Whatever... So... who gave you the disease?"

"Heck if I know. I used to be out of control in my earlier years. That's why I'm so conscious about everything now."

"Well it's a little too late for that, isn't it?"

"I saved your life, didn't I?"

"How dare you say that to me? How dare you?" I said, still screaming.

"I'm serious. I could have slept with you on the first date. Am I wrong about that?"

"I can't believe you. Didn't you say you had a wife and a six-year-old son? What happened to them?"

"She walked in on me and my best friend in our bed."

"What? Kenny that is so foul!"

"Yeah, I know, but I couldn't help it. It's a whole different world on the other side, nothing like you've ever experienced. It's exciting, wild, and crazy, especially if you do a couple of lines first."

"Lines, you do drugs too? Damn!"

"I don't anymore. That was way back then."

"So, you screwed a dude in the bed that you shared with your wife?"

"Unfortunately,"

"Had you done it before and just hadn't gotten caught?"

"You could say that."

"Where is she now?"

"Her and my son lives in New Orleans East. We went to court when she divorced me and she told the judge what she saw. She demanded full custody and won, but I do get to see him every other Saturday."

"What does she think about all of this?"

"She said that she never wants to see me again and she told the judge that I could keep everything in the house. She didn't want anything to do with me, the house or anything in it."

"I can't say that I blame her Kenny. That was nasty what you did. You put her life in jeopardy."

"No she's fine. She's been tested over and over again."

"So? What is that supposed to mean?"

"It means she is perfectly healthy. We had not been intimate with each other for almost a year when I started messing around anyway."

"Well, thank God for that. Were you going to sleep with me?"

"If it were up to me, probably not, but since you wanted it so bad, I might have, but we would've used a condom."

"Kenny, are you kidding me? Condoms break! How dare you! I can't believe this. I feel really sick right now."

"Reina, contrary to what you think I don't go around giving it to people. I am careful. It's pure hell living with this disease. I wouldn't wish this on my worst enemy."

"Well I should hope not."

"There are tons of medications to take, most of which make you sick to your stomach.

Then there are the side effects like diarrhea, vomiting and sometimes I'm just downright exhausted. Who wants to live like that? I keep telling you that I wouldn't do that to you, Reina."

"Kenny, I have to go. I'm messed up in the head right now, I hope you can understand that and besides I've never actually met an HIV positive person before. If I have I certainly didn't know about it."

"Believe me Reina, I'm sure you have. People don't usually walk around wearing a sign and it's generally not a good ice breaking topic, so how would you know?"

"I would know because hopefully they would have the decency to tell me, unlike you."

"Reina, Reina," he shouted.

I grabbed my purse as fast as I could and ran outside to my car, without turning back. All I could think of was that kiss, that dirty little kiss. I felt like I needed a scalding hot shower to wash away anything he might have given me.

When I walked up to my door, I looked down at the welcome mat and almost stepped on a picture of Lance and me, torn in half. I picked up the piece with Lance's face on it and immediately a wave of guilt came rushing over me like the waves on a beach right before a hurricane.

I figured Mitch was at it again. If I went to file a restraining order against him, Lance would find out about it and that was the last thing on earth that I needed to happen. I called Jeffrey and told him about the latest occurrence. He said he would personally stake out our place to catch Mitch in the act the next time he came prowling. The only problem was that Jeffrey had to be at the police station for desk duty five days out of the week, so I did not know how much good it would really do, but it was worth the effort and besides, he agreed to keep quiet.

I tried to relax my mind, but it was running a mile a minute. Immediately, I brushed my teeth, scrubbed my tongue and then jumped in the shower and disinfected my body for a good half hour until my skin turned red and still, I did not feel clean enough. Even though I did not have sex with him, the thought of being that close to him made me ill. The idea of knowing that in a matter of minutes, I could have contracted a fatal disease for the rest of my life scared me senseless.

I fell onto my knees and prayed to God that he would protect me from the devil, which was obviously trying to swallow me up. After my thirty minute prayer, I went on line to look up the AIDS virus to make sure that I wasn't coming down with any of the symptoms, which I was sure was premature, but I needed some facts.

I just could not believe that I had gone on three dates with three different guys and all of them had serious issues. Donovan had a live in lover whom he secretly shared a child with, Mitch was a compulsive player and dangerously psychotic, and Kenny, he was on the down-low, walking around with a fatal disease.

Having experienced the single life reopened my eyes. I always knew that it was crazy out there, but to experience it for myself made me want my husband back.

I just needed to make things right with my Lance. I needed to figure out a way to be happy and content with what I had at home because there was nothing out there in those streets except deceit, disappointment and diseases. I was convinced that Lance and I could make our relationship work, now more than ever. I guess I just had to get out there and see for myself. I could speak firsthand about the idea of the grass seeming greener on the other side. It wasn't.

# Chapter 16

I didn't sleep much during the night and woke up earlier than usual this morning; three-twelve to be exact. My body shook from anxiety. I sat up in the bed thinking about last night at Kenny's house. I was still very upset and worried. I looked over to see Lance, still fast asleep. I felt so empty and alone. I had shunned my husband for strange men, who just used me as a play toy.

A few hours later, after Lance left for work, the doorbell rang. I answered, but no one was there. There was a large anonymous manila envelope stuffed into the mail slot. I pulled it out and looked at it very closely. There was no name or return address. I took it into the downstairs bathroom to have some privacy in case Lance back-tracked home for any reason. I slowly peeled away the glue and pulled out twelve photos. I looked at them one by one, in disbelief. I almost died when I saw myself at the restaurant with Donovan and in the park holding hands with Mitch. The icing on the cake was the video tape that I slid into the bedroom video cassette player, which was of Kenny and me at his house. All of the intimate things that we had done became nakedly exposed. Someone even took the initiative to go as far as to edit the tape, so that certain parts played in slow motion.

I felt light headed, as if I were going to pass out. Time was at a standstill and I could not prevent the horror that overtook me. My brain raced faster than NASCAR. My mind struggled to figure out who would be tailing me and why. Somebody had some major dirt on me and I needed to find out who was behind it.

My life was falling apart right in front of my own eyes and I felt helpless. This was out of control. I looked around for a brown paper bag in the kitchen. I felt myself hyperventilating.

I had not seen or heard from Mitch since the incident, but he was still a suspect, as far as I was concerned. I thought I might just have to call the police and make up a bogus story to tell Lance.

I dialed 911 and told them that I had a stalker type situation. They said, they would send someone out to speak with me. When they arrived, I told them that this guy Mitch asked me out on a date and I refused, so he started following me around and coming to my house. They asked me some real tough questions, some of which I had to answer on the spot and utilize my quick thinking skills. They wanted to know how I knew him, where we met, and how he knew where I lived. They also asked me if he and I had any intimate dealings. I lied right through my teeth.

They said, I could press charges against him and they would bring him in for questioning. I agreed. The officer also recommended that I get a restraining order against him for protection. Even though the stress was getting to me, I felt as if I had done the right thing.

Lance came running through the door when he saw the police cars outside of the house. He started asking me if I was okay. I was scared to death. I just knew he would see right through me, if my story was not concrete. It added to my stress level to have to make one up and put it all together as I went along, not to mention remembering it in case I was asked again later.

The officer said, he was leaving and for me to get that restraining order first thing in the morning. I said I would. He left after taking my statement and then Lance chimed in with all of his questions.

I said, Mitch was a psychotic guy who wouldn't take no, for an answer. That was it concisely. Lance was supportive. He said, I did not need to get a restraining order against Mitch. He threatened that if he ever caught him on our property, he would blow his head off. Lance was not a violent person, but I was seeing a different side of him that I had never seen before. He was so upset; he talked about sleeping on the sofa, so that he would be right at the front door if Mitch came back.

I knew in my heart that I had messed up for real this time. Usually I was so smooth but this time, I was careless and negligent. I was even disappointed in myself. That was a first.

I went to bed and tried to fall asleep, but I just couldn't stop thinking about what Mitch might do next. This could potentially turn out bad. I did not want anything to happen to Lance while trying to protect me. I was worried that Mitch was getting bolder by the minute.

I thought of calling him to see where his head was. Maybe if I would call him to apologize he would forget about it. Whatever trip this man was on was affecting my whole life and I did not like it one bit.

While I lay in bed, my phone rang from a restricted caller. I quietly answered, "hello', but there was no answer on the other end. I said, hello five or six times and then pressed the end button on my cell.

I must have fallen asleep. Before I knew it, it was morning. Lance had never come to bed. I went down to check on him but he was already gone for the day. In a way, I was glad so I didn't have to answer any more redundant questions. Lance was clever. I knew I had to be careful not to tip him off.

As a last result, I called Seth and the crew to come down to pay Mitch a visit. Even though they were not young men anymore, they would still serve their purpose. I hated to do that because I would not be responsible for the outcome. I hated the thought of the type of violence that I knew Seth would resort to, but my back was up against the wall and I needed Mitch gone for good. He was causing too much trouble for me.

Seth was talking to me holding his cell phone on his left ear while on the phone booking a flight on his right ear. Once I summoned them, I knew there was no turning back, but I had made it up in my mind to let Seth take care of it. A restraining order was a joke and the police officer looked suspicious of me, so this was my last and only hope.

Six hours later, I received a knock on my door. It was Seth and his boy Buns. They were in Atlanta taking care of business when I called with my drama. By the time they arrived, I had bitten off eight of my ten false nails, out of nervousness. I told Seth everything I knew about Mitch, what he looked like, where the studio was and everything.

Seth went about his mission, called me from the road, and told me that everything had been taken care of and for me not to worry. I wanted details, but he said, if I don't know anything, I could not tell anything. There he was protecting me again, just like old times.

Lance came home early from work and offered to cook dinner, since I seemed so stressed out. I accepted. We ate our tacos and sat in silence for the rest of the evening. I was exhausted.

# Chapter 17

I opened my eyes at precisely *three-twelve,* as I had done for the last few days. I was starting to think there was some significance to those numbers. It rather frightened me because I knew deep down that there had to be a reason for it. I felt like that particular time was vital; I just didn't know what it could have meant. I heard a preacher say once, that God speaks to you between three and five in the morning and I was listening intently.

A few hours later, my boss called and said that she needed to have a very important meeting with me immediately. I hurriedly threw some clothes on and dashed out the door. It sounded important. I figured that there must have been a mix up with one of my furniture orders, especially for her to call so early.

I jumped in my car and took off in route to the nearest gas station. I grabbed a lottery ticket and a hot cup of coffee to help me cope with whatever, once I arrived at the store. On my way, I saw what looked like pictures of me plastered on a wooden light post. I slowed down and pulled closer to the neutral ground. Sure enough, there Donovan was feeding me, holding hands with Mitch and dry humping Kenny. The photos exhibited even more explicit sightings of me doing things that I wanted to forget, but visibly was not able to.

I hastily hopped out of my car and ran over to the tell-tale post to tear them all down. There were seven of them. My feelings were so hurt. I was speechless. I started ripping them up into tiny little pieces and throwing them on the ground. Cars were passing by looking at me with disapproving stares. I was humiliated. I got in my car, drove a little further to run across another light post full of a different set of photos. I screeched, jumped out and ripped those up too. I drove to the next stop light to find them there as well. I retrieved them and moved forward hoping to God that there would not be anymore. This had to be it, I thought. I couldn't imagine Mitch taking the time to go around the entire city posting up pictures.

I looked at my watch to keep track of how much time I had wasted, when I was supposed to have been at my meeting. I walked through the door and everyone had strange looks on their faces. They were not as playful as usual. I suspected that something was wrong. I went into the back office, sat down in the chair in front of the desk, and exhaled.

Ms. Charlene's short legs swung back and forth without hitting the floor as she sat in her executive chair behind the desk, just looking at me not saying a word. She had in her hand the exact same manila envelope that arrived at my home. I freaked out and started stuttering. I tried to explain myself. She wasn't listening to anything I was saying. All she knew was that I was cheating on Lance, who was like a son to her. Lance had assisted her with whatever she needed throughout the years, which was why she gave me this job in the first place. She was initially leery of me because my degree was in sociology, which had absolutely nothing to do with furniture.

She asked me to clean off my desk and not to return. All that I could do was oblige her wishes. I felt terrible like a total loser. It was a real blow to my ego.

I sat in my car out back, next to the company moving trucks for three hours before I left the parking lot to head home. I just could not face Lance. How was I supposed to tell him that I lost my job and why? For all I knew she would probably tell him herself.

I made it home, finally. I sat in my car for another half hour to think and then proceeded to go inside. As I approached the walkway, I saw the words "whore, slut, bitch," written in big bold black letters all over my door. At this point, the element of surprise was inevitable. I quickly looked inside of our tool shed to get one of Lance's solvents to remove the profane words. I was able to remove most of it but there were still traces of black smudges from the magic marker leftover. I hopped back in my car and drove to the Hardware store to buy something stronger to scrub it, without removing the paint. I hurried to beat Lance home. He had been coming straight home from work, trying to catch Mitch in the act.

I made it back home, scrubbed the door until I saw that there was no hint of evidence left. I stepped inside for the first time since this morning. I went into the kitchen to grab a glass of Remy Red to put me at ease. I headed up the freshly shampooed carpeted stairs to use the bathroom. When I got there, I noticed that his shaving kit was gone. I found that strange, so I looked in the closet to discover all of his shower essentials gone. I called his cell phone, but he did not answer. I tried five consecutive times, to no avail, which told me he was intentionally avoiding my calls. I walked all around the condominiums to see what else was missing, everything to put it mildly.

After realizing, the possibility that Lance may have moved out, I freaked. Tears began to stream down my face. I stood motionless in the middle of the room. I ran into the bedroom closet, opened the door and all of his clothes were gone. His whole side was completely bare. I frantically pulled my cell phone out of my purse and tried calling him again. I didn't know what was happening. I wondered if Ms. Charlene had gotten to him already. Maybe he saw the posters on one of the poles.

I did not understand why Mitch would go to so much trouble to get revenge. I started thinking long and hard about it and concluded that Mitch could not have written those words on the door because Uncle Seth said he took care of him, whatever that meant. It had to be someone else, but who? I did not have any enemies, that I knew about.

I tussled back and forth in my mind, going over every event that has transpired in the past month. I fully intended to win Lance back somehow. I knew that I had screwed up and I was sure at some point he would run across the incriminating evidence so I had better start thinking of a plan to get out of it.

I went through my cell looking for numbers of a few of his friends. I called three of his boys to see if they had heard from him. They said that they had not, but it's not like I expected them to be truthful if they did. That was probably a waste of time. I wondered what was going through Lance's head. I wondered if I should even feel safe enough to fall asleep, if I was even able to sleep.

I went back down to the kitchen to grab the shank knife that Uncle Seth had given me the last time I saw him, and put it under my pillow, just in case Lance came home in the middle of the night with something on his mind. I had to be prepared.

It became dark in the room. The sun started to set. I lit a few candles around the house, took off my clothes, locked the bathroom door, and shampooed my hair.

I heard the house phone ringing. I jumped out of the tub, sopping wet but caught it just in time. I kept saying hello but it was dead silence on the other end and then they hung up without saying a word. I finished my shower and then climbed into bed. It was still early, but I needed to lie down for while.

Before I knew it, morning loomed. I rose on my feet as if nothing had happened last night.

I had an attitude. Even though I was the one who messed up, I guess I felt like Lance could have talked to me about it, instead of just leaving. Then I thought, what would I do if I were in his shoes?

I decided that I would just cross Lance's bridge when I came to it. I was dressed and headed to the gas station to put gas in my car and then buy a few items from the grocery store. I did not have any cash on me, just my credit cards. The woman in the store told me that my card declined. I pulled out my back up card and handed it to her. That one declined too. I cringed in disbelief.

I went inside the bank to withdraw some cash manually, to get me through the week and the teller informed me that I had insufficient funds. I argued that she was wrong and made her recheck the information. She confirmed my worst fear. Lance had taken all of the money out of our joint account. He left only one dollar, enough to keep the account open. It took everything within me not to have a screaming fit.

I angrily left the bank and headed back home. I tried my best to be strong and I told myself that I would not cry another tear. I always heard people talk about "mind over matter" so I wanted to see if it would work for me. I said to myself repeatedly, "I am strong and I will overcome this."

I tried to turn the television on, only it didn't come on. I shook the remote and even took the batteries out. When nothing happened, I got up, walked over to it, and manually tried to turn it on, nothing. I hit the light switch to see if the lights would come on, they did not.

I called the electric company to report the outage. They told me that the bill hasn't been paid. I asked if the disconnection was due to nonpayment or if the account had been closed. The raspy voiced woman informed me that she could not disclose any information unless I knew the password that was on the account. I snappily responded that I was Mrs. Joseph and I should be able to have access to the account, as well as Lance. She still would not cooperate.

I was starting to regret not being more involved with the bills. Lance usually took care of all of that stuff. I never even saw them.

The bedroom was extremely hot, almost smothering and reminded me of the sauna at the gym. It had to be a hundred degrees outside, with elevated humidity. I opened all of the windows in the room hoping to get a breeze through the screens. I peeled off my jeans that felt like they were super glued to my legs. I went downstairs and sat on the fawn leather sectional to cool off in just my granny panties because all of my thongs were dirty, but even that was uncomfortable. My skin was stuck to the couch, as I tried to get up to go to the refrigerator, to get some ice water, forgetting that the power was off. All of the meat that was in the freezer was bound to spoil. I had no way of paying that bill.

I called Kayla to see if I could occupy her guest room for few days, until I figured out my next move. I hate asking people for help, because I'm a diva and divas don't ask for favors.

I put my pride on the side and called my friend. She agreed to let me stay there as long as I needed to, so I packed a couple of bags, put Rose in her fluffy carry-on and headed to her house. She informed me that she was packing as we spoke to take a quick business trip to Chicago, but she would be back in town in a couple of days.

On the drive over, I was in total shock that this was happening to me. I never thought no matter what I did that Lance would stoop so low. I thought I had him wrapped around my finger, but I suppose everybody has their breaking point.

I kept looking in the rear view mirror to see if someone was following me. I would not be surprised if Lance had a private investigator tailing me. I refused to cry. I refused to let it get the best of me. I was going to be strong if it killed me.

I pulled up to Kayla's and parked on the street right in front of her house. Her front door was open wide, so I pulled the screen and let myself in. Kayla was running around the house grabbing this and that while Luther sat on the couch watching her.

I asked her if she needed any help, because she looked distressed. She told me to go into the bathroom to grab her loofah sponge. I felt compelled to hurry, since she undoubtedly was worried. She did not want to miss her flight.

Luther decided to get up and help her bring her bags to the car. I watched him take his sweet time, dragging his knuckles and thought to myself, "what a loser."

She kissed him on the cheek, said bye to me, jumped in her car, and then sped off down the street. I stood on the porch for a few minutes, watching the streetcars pass by, as I contemplated what I was going to do next.

Luther offered me an Orange Julius drink. I took him up on it because I needed some kind of fix. My nerves were rattled. We sat in the living room watching a little television, but in fact, the television watched me. I told Kayla I only needed to stay for a couple of days, so I tried to focus on a plan to keep my word. I found it difficult to make one because I had not heard from Lance. I needed to know what his plan was before I could make mine.

Luther kicked his dirty tennis shoes off onto the deep coffee color stained hardwood floor and asked me if I wanted to take mine off. I thought about it for a couple of seconds and then replied, "No thanks."

After he finished his cold drink, he said that he was going to take a shower. I sat there in front of the television with my cell phone in my hand pondering whether to call Lance again. I did not want to give him any more power than he already had, but I was in the wrong, so I felt it was up to me to make the first move. I didn't know whether to just come clean and apologize or try to twist things around. There was only so much twisting that I could do because the proof was in the pictures.

Luther came out of the shower still semi-wet with tiny water beads dripping down his back to his towel wrapped waist. I thought that was a bit odd, but I did not say anything; after all, he did live there. He sat right back in the same spot on the sofa where he was before, with his legs wide open. He picked up the remote and asked me if I wanted to watch anything in particular and I didn't, so he scrolled through the channels.

I laid my head back into the cushions of the sofa looking up at the high ceiling to avoid having to look at him when he stated that there was nothing on television worth watching because it was too early in the morning. The next thing I know he popped in a videocassette tape. I did not think anything of it at first, but when I saw the title, *Black Wet Butts*, I knew something was up. I asked him what he was doing and he said, he watches these videos all the time. I sat there for a couple of minutes trying to figure out his angle. I wasn't sure if he was trying to come on to me or if he was just entertaining himself. Whatever he was doing, I was starting to feel very uncomfortable. He was out of order, to say the very least.

"Luther, I don't want to watch a pornographic movie! Can we watch something else please?"

"I asked you if you wanted to watch something, you said, you didn't care what we watch."

"Yeah, but I didn't mean I wanted to watch porn."

"Aight, let me just watch this one and then we can change it." He said, reaching under the sofa, grabbing a plate of weed.

"No, change it now!"

"It ain't that long girl, stop trippin." He said shuffling around his party favors with a pack of 5.0 papers.

"But it's making me feel uncomfortable."

"Stop being square, me and Kayla watch em all the time."

"That's you and Kayla. She's not here now. You honestly don't feel that this is inappropriate, for real?"

"Inappropriate, how?"

"Because you are sitting here in front of me, in a bath towel with your legs sprawled wide open, watching a porno flick and smoking weed."

"You got it all wrong. This is what I do all the time. Why I gotta change just cause you here? This is my house and if I want to walk around naked in my own house I should be able to do just that."

"You have no class Luther, none what so ever."

"No, you think you all that. You need to chill and just relax a little bit. Ain't nobody thinking about you and your stuck up ass."

"I bet you wouldn't be acting like this if Kayla was here."

"I bet I would."

"I don't know why she puts up with your trifling ass."

"No, I don't know why she think you her homegirl. Ya'll ain't nothing alike. Kayla ain't all uppity like you."

"I'm not uppity, but I do have class, unlike you."

"You ain't gonna keep insulting me in my own house."

"This is not your house. You're lucky my girl lets you stay here. Don't forget where you came from, the projects, remember?"

"Bitch, you don't know nuttin bout me."

"I know all I need to know jailbird, I'm leaving."

I ran up to the guest room, grabbed my overnight bags, and dodged to the door as quickly as I could, trying to get as far away from him as I possibly could.

"Bye bitch," he snarled.

"Your grandma's a bitch," I shouted, as I slammed the door shut.

I do not know what I was thinking, leaving Kayla's house. I had nowhere else to go. As I pulled up to my condo, I sat in the parking lot with Gina's number on speed dial, ready to press the send button. I hesitated, because I was too ashamed to call her and tell her that Lance left me and I put myself in exactly the same situation that she warned me about when we talked about it in New York. I was humiliated that I had not been smart enough to have a backup plan.

I walked in the front door and quickly remembered why I left in the first place. My stomach was in knots. I went into the bathroom and sat on the toilet. I needed to have a serious bowel movement. When I finished, I flushed the toilet and then I realized that the water was not filling back up in the bowl. That was my last flush. Lance must have turned the water off too. Sweet Jesus!

# Chapter 18

I woke up and realized that two long days of me being in that, hot stinky house had gone by and I had barely eaten. Rose was still eating very well though, because I had just bought her a big bag of food that she barely put a dent into. All of the meat and veggies in the refrigerator was spoiled. I was tired of eating canned goods and saltine crackers. I had to do something fast. I had not taken a shower or brushed my teeth, only gargled with mouthwash but it was just not enough. I stank badly. My menstrual cycle flowed. There was nothing for me to use to wash up. I even found a track mark in my granny panties that I wore for the past three days. That was what did it for me. I peeked outside the blinds in the kitchen to see if old Ms. Johnson was outside watering her flowers, as she did every morning and there she was, on her lawn in her robe and flat strapped sandals, right on cue. I tucked a super plus tampon in the front pocket of my jeans. I walked over to her and started up a conversation so that she would invite me inside for some tea or something, then I could lure myself into her bathroom to wash myself up.

"Hi, Ms. Johnson," I smiled and waved, as I walked toward her.
"Oh hello sugah,"
"I've been meaning to come over and visit with you sometime."
"Awe, aren't you just the sweetest thing."
"Well if you aren't busy, I thought we could have some tea?"
"Oh, sure that would be real nice," she smiled.
"Great," I smiled back.

"Well I can finish watering my lawn a little later. I guess that would be okay, but I need to have it done by the time James gets home from work. Come on in sugah," she said, inviting me in.

I let Rose lick the water from the wet leaves in her front lawn and then brought her back inside.

I was elated. We went inside and she escorted me to the kitchen table. I sat there while she put the teapot on. My stomach was about to bust. It was making that rumbling sound when you have to use the bathroom. I was squeezing my muscles trying to muffle the sounds, but it wasn't helping much.

"Ooh honey, are you hungry? Your stomach is growling. I can hear it all the way over here," she teased.

"I always wake up hungry," laughing along with her.

"Let me fix you something to eat. I have oatmeal and toast," she kindly offered.

"Oh no ma'am, I don't want to be any trouble," knowing I wanted some.

"It's no trouble at all. I don't have much since James died, just living off of my fixed income, ya know?"

"Yes ma'am."

I was very confused; she kept going back and forth about her husband James being dead but coming home from work later. I wasn't sure what to think of it. For the first time in my life, I actually felt bad for someone else, instead of only thinking of myself. Poor Ms. Johnson did not have much family. She never had any children. Her husband died late last year and her only living relative was her sickly sister who lived out of town in a nursing home. It was the saddest story I think I had ever heard. I felt even worse that I had not visited with her sooner, especially since she seemed to have the Alzheimer's illness.

I ate my oatmeal, toast and drank my tea. She looked at me with a loving stare. I could not help but wonder if she was suspicious of me; wondering why I was sitting in her kitchen. I put that thought on the back burner and started thinking of how I would weasel my way into her bathroom.

"May I use your restroom Ms. Johnson? This tea is running straight through me," I lied.

"Sure you can, first door on the right sugah," she chuckled.

I excused myself, locking the door behind me. I could hear her talking to her beloved Mr. James. It was somewhat scary; but I had to deal with issues that were more pressing at the time. I went into the bathroom cabinet and grabbed a towel to put on the floor, snug against the bottom of the door to prevent any smells from escaping out into the hall. I sat there and slowly squeezed out piece by piece in an effort to keep quiet. I tried extremely hard to keep all sounds to a minimum.

When I finished, I grabbed the air freshener spray from the side of the bathtub, turned the water on, and squirted a little at a time. I didn't want her to know what I had done in her bathroom.

I took the towels up, refolded them, and put them back in the closet. They smelled like mothballs. I felt bad about doing that, but I had to keep her unaware.

I went back in the kitchen and sat down. My body felt so much better, but emotionally, I was a wreck. I told her what a nice visit I had and that we should do it again very soon. She agreed and invited me back anytime. I gave her a hug and then walked back to the condo.

My days seemed so long. I pulled out a book and brought it out to the back patio where I sat for most of the day. It was cooler than being in the house. Kayla had been trying to call me but I didn't know what to say to her. I did not want to start trouble between her and Luther so I figured it would just be better to keep my mouth shut for a while. She already knew how he was and she always took him back. I did not want to risk us falling out over that creep, so I just ignored her calls for the time being.

I called Gina to feel her out and see if she would let me stay with her for a while. Maybe I could get a job in New York and eventually get my own place.

"Gina?"

"Hey Reina, how are you?"

"Oh, I'm fine, just thought I'd give you a call today."

"Well that's sweet. You were thinking of me huh?"

"Always Gee, always."

"Cool, what's up with you?"

"Oh nothing much; Lance and I had a fight, that's all"

"Girl, you and that man stay at it, don't you?'

Gina started teasing me and making light of the situation. I did not know how to tell her that he had moved out.

"Yeah, I guess we do."

"You guys will work it out Reina, you always do."

"I don't know girl, this time might be different. He was really mad at me."

"Just pray about it. God will work it out for you. You just have to trust him Reina."

"Yeah, that's good advice, as always. What you doing this weekend, feel like some company?"

"I am not going to let you keep running away from your problems Reina. Girl, you have to stay there and stick it out with him. That's what marriage is all about. Remember our talk the last time you were here?"

"Yep, I remember."

"Alright then, no more running, okay?"

"Yeah, I hear you girl."

"Okay good. Call me later because I'm running late for my doctor's appointment. I'm going to get my yearly pap and make sure my IUD is still working, talk to you later girl." She chuckled.

"Okay, talk to you later."

After hanging up with Gina, I cried. I realized that the conversation did not go as I had planned and I was disappointed that she did not ask me to come there, but at least I still had a little bit of pride left. I made sure I did not grovel, but I couldn't stop the tears from running down my face.

I bent down on my knees to pray, as Gina recommended. It felt a little awkward knowing that I had brought all of this upon myself. Why would God want to help me out of this one?

My cell phone rang and it was again from an unavailable number. I answered it.

"Hello," trying not to sound distressed.

No one replied.

"Hello," said the man on the other end.

"Is this Reina?"

"Yes, who is this?"

"You don't know me, but I know you."

"Okay, so what's your name?"

"You don't need to know all of that Ms. Thing."

"Well what do you want?"

"We have a mutual friend."

"Who are you talking about, because I don't have time for any stupid games?"

"Look, you are not calling any shots here Ms. Girl. You just stay the hell away from Kenneth."

"Okay, who the hell is this?"

"You just stay away, consider yourself warned."

"Oh hell no, you don't have to worry about me seeing or talking to Kenny anymore. I'm done with him. He better not ever call my phone again and believe me if you knew what I know you'd stay away too."

"Let me tell you something Ms. Fish, there is nothing that I don't know about my man, okay. We share everything."

"Well good for you and I'd appreciate it if you would stop prank calling my phone."

"I was just having a little fun, that's all. Did you like the photos I sent you?"

"You bastard, you posted up all of those pictures?"

"Sure I did. Who did you think did it, your husband; by the way, how is Lance anyway? Please send him my love."

"You asshole, you better stay the hell away from my husband. I told you Kenny and I are through, now leave us alone!" I screamed.

"Oh that's quite fine with me, besides my job here is done anyway. Have a nice life, Ms. Tuna fish."

I hung up the phone and sat there pissed off, brewing. I wanted to ring his damn neck. There was just one problem; I didn't know who he was.

I went back and forth in my mind about asking Ms. Johnson if I could spend the night at her condo without alerting her of what was really going on. I was quite embarrassed about my situation. I didn't want anyone and I meant anyone at all to know, not even my dearest friends. I had to keep up appearances, even to them. I knew they loved me, but I was sure somewhere in the back of their minds they thought I was a spoiled brat and took Lance for granted. I did not need to hear those words fall out of either Gina or Kayla's mouth. I couldn't handle it. I just couldn't handle my closest friends thinking that I was a failure. I looked in the yellow pages to find a shelter for the night. Having to sleep one more night in that hot house, would have been unbearable. I slept completely naked and still could not get any relief. The windows were all open but there was no breeze; typical New Orleans weather, unlike, most cities where the temperature drops at night.

I looked all around the house and gathered up as much change as I could find, gritted my teeth and headed for the bus stop. I was on my way to a shelter for the night. No one would ever know I was there unless I told them and that would never happen in a million years, so off I went.

On the ride to my destination, I had second thoughts as well as thirds and fourths but it was too late. I had adamantly made up my mind. I was not spending another night in that hot house, period. I didn't want anyone to find me dead in the morning, due to dehydration or heat exhaustion.

When I arrived at the shelter, there were all of these women and children standing outside waiting to get in the building. I hurriedly secured myself a place in line, since I overheard the women talking about how they hoped there would be enough beds for them and their kids. Some of the women looked as if they stayed in shelters on a regular basis. They had the routine down to a science. Some of them assembled in cliques. They stood together as if they were best friends carousing at a cook out. I felt out of place.

Cars passed up and down the street and each time I would turn my head away from the street, just in case someone drove by that I knew. If someone were to ask what my most embarrassing moment in life was, I would have to say, spending the night in a homeless shelter was definitely second runner up. The absolute most embarrassing would be the time I walked out of the bathroom in church with my skirt tucked in my stockings. My whole rear was exposed. Sister Brown pulled me to the side and told me. I was mortified.

Finally, I was inside. Initially I smelled Lysol but my stomach turned at the strong stench of musty armpits and female body odor that penetrated through the open space. It reminded me of the raunchy strip club I worked at in college, as a cashier.

A female guard told us to choose a bed. I picked one toward the end of the room. I stood next to it for a couple of minutes until I decided to sit on the very edge. I watched the women entering the building with their children. It was the saddest thing I had ever seen. I almost forgot about myself for a moment and felt bad for them, until a butch-looking female came up to me demanding that I relinquish her bed.

"You're in my bed," she told me.

"There's no name on these beds," I replied.

"I always sleep here, so move it!"

"Are you serious?"

She threw her cruddy knapsack on the bed and sat down next to me, staring into my eyes.

"I guess it's big enough for the both of us then."

She lay on her back with her head in her palms and elbows in the air, still staring at me, not saying a word.

I got up, snatched my bag and moved to an empty bed on the other side of the room. It sat right in between two women who were having a conversation with one another. One talked about how she found the shelter to be an upgrade from her previous prison cell and the other one said she was on the run from her husband who beat her every chance he got.

It was lights out at ten o clock. I couldn't sleep. I tried to stay alert incase the lesbian chick came for me after the lights went off. After hours and hours of listening to moans and snores, I must have unwillingly drifted off. The best part was the air conditioning. I was not hot, but instead cold. I covered up with the thin, rough woven blanket and before I knew it, it was morning.

I waited for the bus and rode off into the suburbs. A place I knew well and felt most comfortable.

# Chapter 19

I broke down and called my Aunt Betty, after all, she was family. I wanted to feel her out to see if I could visit with them for a while. I needed somewhere to lay my head comfortably. I did not know how comfortable it would be but at least she had electricity, water, and plenty of food.

She did not ask any questions, just told me that I was always welcome to come there any time I wanted. I hung up the phone with her and went directly to my jewelry box to find something to pawn, so that I could gather up enough money for a plane ticket.

Since the electricity was off, I decided to go to the library to use the computer to check out the fares. I jumped in my car, started driving, but only made it about a mile down the road when I ran out of gas. I didn't have enough gas to even make it two miles to the library but I was determined not to spend one more night in that house. I left the car on the side of the road and walked the rest of the way, which was about another mile. That was the longest mile of my life especially since my heel broke off my left sandal.

I walked barefoot into the library. A very tall and skinny lady with a snooty attitude stopped me at the door. She said that I had to put my shoes back on. I told the young woman that I had broken my heel, so she let me come in and use the computer, as long as I stayed in my seat and did not walk around. She informed me that it was a liability issue.

All of the airlines were comparable in price and they were all out of my league, almost three hundred dollars just to get to Mississippi because it was such short notice. That was outrageous. I looked at the Greyhound fares, just to see what tickets were going for and surprisingly they were significantly cheaper. I always said that I would never ride a bus but I had exhausted every option, besides that and hitch-hiking.

A dark skinned guy with slender facial features sitting at one of the other computers kept giving me the eye. I acted as if I did not see him because I was in no condition to be fraternizing. He got up and came over to me because he saw that I was about to leave.

"What's your name?"

"Reina," I replied dryly.

"You sexy," he told me, licking his lips.

"Thanks," I replied, walking towards the exit.

"I wanna get to know you,"

"Why?" I quizzed.

"Cause, you sexy like I said," he responded in his thug lingo.

"I'm sorry but I'm not interested,"

"I just wanna be your friend ma," he said, rubbing the top of his baldhead, following me to the door.

"I have enough friends."

"You could never have enough friends," he said. "Let me take you out and show you a good time."

"You don't have enough money to take me out and show me a good time," I frowned.

"Aight, that's cool. I like that, you bout cho dough huh?" he asked, pulling out a large roll of hundred dollar bills.

"Damn! What do you do?" I asked, curiously.

"Imma bidnessman baby," he said, with a straight face.

"Humn, I don't know," thinking of how I must have looked and even smelled.

"Why you trippin, my pockets are fat and its mo where dat came from, so waz up lil shorty?"

"What do you mean?" I asked, looking down at the knot.

"It's on you ma. You tell me waz up? You wanna get soma dis?"

"I don't know, but I sure could use some right about now," I said, getting excited.

"Meet me at dat Howard Johnson's on the Expressway in about a hour. Imma be there waitin on you."

"Hell yeah," I thought to myself. Women do this all the time. I tried to convince myself not to think about it and just do it, how bad could it possibly be; at least he was half-way cute. Many women give their body away free, so why not be paid for it? Although I knew it was wrong, I needed money badly. I tossed the idea around in my head trying to convince myself that it was not that bad to sell your body for money, but I knew better. Both my grandmothers' Whila Mae and Big Mama would roll over in their graves if they could see me now. They did not raise me to be a prostitute, but I had to do what I had to do.

As I walked home barefoot, I felt something sticking me in the bottom of my foot. It was a piece of glass. I tried to pull it out standing up, but I kept losing my balance so I sat down on the sidewalk and dug until it came out. I finally made it back home and soaked my foot in peroxide.

I grabbed my favorite tennis bracelet that Lance bought me for my Birthday the first year that we were together. I was torn whether to sell it or not. I really loved that bracelet. It was sentimental to me, but I needed this money and I would probably get the most for it than any other piece I owned. I put my tennis shoes on and walked to the pawnshop that was luckily right down the street from our condo. I felt horrible when it was time to hand over my bracelet. I wanted to cry until the guy behind the counter said that I could later buy it back from him. I took the money and went back home to pack.

I was second-guessing my decision to trick myself for a few hundred dollars but I needed money quick. I knew if this guy was willing to throw money at me, I could work it so good I could easily end up with a thousand.

I took ten dollars out of the money from the pawnshop and caught a taxi to the hotel. I knew I would be able to replenish it with my earnings from my gig.

I caught the elevator up to the fifth floor and knocked on the door, there he stood in his Calvin Klein boxer shorts waiting for me to arrive. He was a handsome chocolate man with no facial hair and a no-nonsense look about him. I didn't even know his name and did not find it necessary to ask. I was there for one reason and one reason only, to get my money.

I asked if I could use the shower and he obliged. I turned the hot water on and jumped in. A hot shower never felt so good. It was weird for me to have to use a tiny bar of scentless soap but it was surely better than nothing was at all. I made the most of it. It felt great.

As soon as I walked out of the tiny bathroom, he rolled a condom on, ripped my clothes off, and roughly threw me on the bed. I let him ravish me to no end. I never thought that I would be selling my body for money, especially after turning my nose up at other women who had done the same thing. Maybe it was just in my blood.

I pretended that I was making love to Lance so that I would have the strength to get through it. I in turn jumped on top of him, closed my eyes, and rode him like an award winning horse at the racetrack. I tried to emulate what the women were doing on the porno that Luther showed me. He moaned and grunted, grunted and moaned. He tugged my hair I had pulled back into a ponytail, spanked me until my butt turned bright red, and called me a couple of bitches and hoes but I didn't care. I knew that when it was all over, I would leave there in a better situation than I came.

When it was all over, we both laid face up, panting and looking at the plain white ceiling.

"Aight, you gon have to roll now ma," he said, abruptly.

I took a minute to think about the fact that he wanted me to leave so quickly and felt insulted.

"Okay, I'll go. You got what you say you had for me?" I asked.

"What's that?" he asked, perplexed.

"What do you mean? I'm talking about my money," I said, irritated.

"I had to test out the goods first before I put you to work ma, but I ain't payin fo nothin, you pay me after you get paid," he said, in a firm tone.

"What? You said you were going to give me a few hundred dollars, remember?" I said, standing there naked.

"Naw, I don't remember no shit like dat ma, fo real. You wanna work or not? This is a

misunderstandin or sumthin, I don't pay fo no pussy," he exclaimed.

"You're kidding right?" I said, putting my clothes back on.

"Hell naw. You either gon let me put you to work or you gots to roll out ma, fo real. Time is money. Just like you bout yours, I'm damn sho bout mines. I got a coupla bitches on the way over here right now to bring me my bread, so whatchu gon do?" he asked, walking over to the other side of the bed, reaching down toward the floor.

"Fuck you, mutha fucka. You tryna play me?" I hollered angrily.

"Trick you better get on fo you get yoself hurt."

I hurriedly ran out of the door and took the smoky elevator down to the lobby in disbelief. While on the elevator, I shook in anger. I wanted to kill him. I was full of negative thoughts and wished him much harm and destruction all the way home.

My bus would be coming soon, so I did not have much time to brood. I grabbed my bags and sat them at the front door to wait for my taxi.

I found out that they did not allow animals on the bus. I was devastated and did not know what I was going to do with Rose. I poured all of the food in that big bag onto the kitchen floor so that she could eat at her own discretion. I poured the remaining three gallons of her mineral water into several of her ten inch stainless steel bowls in case she got thirsty. I initially paper trained her when Lance first brought her home to me. I spread the Times Picayune out in the middle of the kitchen floor for when she had to use the bathroom, hoping she would remember to use the paper since she hasn't had to in a long while, because I walk her so often. I planned to come back for her as soon as I could.

My cab was twenty minutes late and he did not apologize. He just dropped me off, right in front of the station and drove away. I walked in and bought my ticket. I had missed the bus that I was supposed to take and ended up having to wait another two hours for the next one. I quietly sat in my seat looking around at all of the grungy people waiting to board. There were babies crying and people lounging on the floor. I was hungry, but I had to save every dime I had so I wouldn't be completely broke when I got to Mississippi.

Finally, it was my turn to board. I toted my three bags to the bus, where an older man threw them under the bottom, along side of all the others. I worried about my Louis Vuitton bags. I had hoped they would be in the same condition that I last saw them.

"Hey, watch the bags, will you?" I expressed, with deep concern.

The older man just looked at me in disgust and continued loading everyone else's, there was nothing I could do about it, except pout and that didn't seem to be doing me any good.

We made three stops, where I had to get off the bus and on different ones before we arrived at my stop. I sat way in the back. I decided to wait until everybody else had gotten off so, I didn't have to fight my way through the crowd. When it came time for me to get my bags, they weren't there. I was the last one left standing, waiting on my luggage. My bags just were not there. I went to the ticket counter and told them that I could not find my bags. They asked me what they looked like and for my ticket stubs. Someone thought that the bags might be on the wrong bus. They agreed to locate them for me. I yelled at the woman behind the counter, telling her how expensive those bags were, not to mention all of my belongings. She calmly took my cell phone number and said that they would call as soon as they found them. I was pissed.

Aunt Betty and Cousin Emma Jean were there waiting for me with opened arms. They were so happy to see me and I was happy to be off that damn bus. They hugged and kissed me, as they did when they saw me for the first time in four years. We hopped in Cousin Emma Jean's pickup truck and headed to the house. I sat squashed in the middle of the two of them, looking through the dusty glass windows. Neither of them questioned the reason for my visit and I was glad for that. We pulled up to the house and Aunt Betty offered me a hot bath. I took her up on it, except I didn't have any clothes to put on when I was finished. Cousin Emma Jean said she would get me something to wear and for me not to worry.

When I finished my bath, I noticed an outfit draped over the top of the door. It was a pair of tight Levi jeans and a terribly unattractive shirt that she said she was giving away to the Good Will, since her granddaughter Lou Ella that was pregnant could not fit them anymore. I put them on and then stood looking at myself in the mirror with skepticism.

Aunt Betty and Cousin Emma Jean were both in the kitchen preparing for a family dinner to celebrate my arrival. When I found that out, I wanted to pretend I was sick, just so that I wouldn't have to see everyone, at least not until I was able to get some better clothes. Before I knew it, people were walking through the garage door, which was always unlocked. For the second time in one month, I had to see my entire family in their rarest form.

I asked if they needed any help with the meal. Cousin Emma Jean handed me a pan and some dinner rolls to butter. I threw them in the oven and then began setting the table.

After dinner, some of my younger cousins wanted to take me out to the juke joint to show me a good time, but I was not in the mood to go anywhere. I was depressed about everything that had gone wrong in the past week and was trying to think up ways to rectify them. I could not come up with anything. My brain was just tired.

It was time for bed and the gathering started to break up, with only a few lingerers left behind. I said that I was going to call it a night. I went into the guest room that Aunt Betty prepared for me and went to sleep.

The next morning Aunt Betty said that Cousin Lou Ella had called after I went to bed, to invite me to go to the movie theatre with her and a few of her friends. I wouldn't have had anything to wear, so I would have had to decline the offer anyway. I attempted to use my cell phone to call the bus station to see what they found out about my bags, but was unable to dial out. The automated voice on the other end said "welcome to Verizon wireless and my call had been intercepted due to nonpayment" or some crap. They may have tried to call me, but could not get through.

I used Aunt Betty's landline to call the number that I found in the yellow pages. They said that they were still in the process of tracking my bags. I argued that they should have given me some compensation, due to the terrible inconvenience they had caused me. I had no clothes, no make-up, underwear, nothing. She said that she needed another day or so to find the bags before we could talk about compensation. I hung up in her face.

Aunt Betty came in my room and offered me to watch the soaps with her, so I went into the living room and sat on the couch next to her, because I did not want to seem ungrateful. I appreciated everything that my family did for me, but honestly, I just didn't want to be bothered. I just wanted to stay to myself, to think and mope if I wanted to. I did not feel like being cordial, having family gatherings, and having to smile when I felt like crying. It was all too overwhelming.

We watched three different soap operas in a row, before I nodded off. The next thing I knew, I looked out of the window and saw her bending down in the backyard flinging around some dirt. Aunt Betty liked to stay busy. It kept her young, she always said. She spotted me watching her and waved her hand for me to come out and join her. We planted seeds hoping to reap a harvest of greens and cabbage. I had never gardened before.

"Reina honey, I don't know what you're going through or why you are even here, but we sure are glad to have you," Aunt Betty expressed, in a tender tone.

"Thank you Aunt Betty, that means a great deal to me. I know I haven't been the best niece and..."

"Nonsense, you are a wonderful niece and we all love you so much," she chimed in, looking me directly in the eyes.

"Well thank you again Aunt Betty," I held my head down in shame.

"Will you be staying awhile honey?"

"I'm not really sure," I answered, honestly.

"Well you are welcomed to stay as long as you like. I hate to see you go," she said.

"I know," I replied, sadly.

We talked awhile and then went into the house to relax, before we made dinner. I had forgotten how much I enjoyed her company.

Almost a week of reconnecting with my family had gone by. I had cooked, gardened, and even sewed a button onto one of Lou Ella's old shirts. The bus station still had not found my bags, which was a mere insult, as well as a sham; I believed someone took my bags.

# Chapter 20

"Lance, thank God you answered. Please don't hang up," I pleaded.

"What Reina? What do you want?" Lance asked, abruptly.

"We need to talk," I urgently proposed.

"We don't have anything to talk about, nothing at all. I know every damn thing I need to know about you," he said, angrily.

"Wait! Hold on a minute. Please let me explain. You don't understand, I was lonely and you were never there and..." I blubbered.

"I don't want to hear that. Don't you dare try to insult my intelligence? You had no right to treat me like this; after all I've done for you?"

"I know Lance, but just listen, please..." I begged.

"I took good care of you and you spit in my face like this?" he asked, sternly.

"Lance, listen, please!" I desperately pleaded.

"I'm selling the condo. I'm here now gathering up the last bit of my things. Your things will be outside so you better come and get them if you want them!" he coldly demanded.

"What? I can't come right now Lance. I'm not even in town."

"One of your boyfriends took you in, huh? You are such a slut. I had no freaking idea that I was married to a dirty slut like you. You really had me fooled. We are over, you hear me? I hope you find whatever it is that you're looking for," he said, unsympathetically.

"Lance please, I didn't mean to hurt you baby," I said, whimpering aloud.

"It's a little late for apologies now. I'm moving on. I'm going to find myself a woman that appreciates a nice guy like me. You can't hurt me anymore Reina. I won't let you," he said, as if he were calming down.

"Baby I need you," I whined.

"Oh now you need me? You didn't need me when you were all hugged up with those other dudes, but you need me now, right?" he condescendingly shouted.

"I didn't even sleep with them Lance, I promise,"

"Well too bad for you because I don't give a damn. You should've slept with them then maybe you would've at least gotten a nut out of the deal. Now you have nothing you stupid cunt," he said, callously.

"Lance, why are you calling me names? I'm trying to explain, baby please..."

"Your bags will be out by the dumpsters when you get here. I've already changed the locks."

"Lance, wait a minute. You can't just throw all of my stuff in the garbage. That's illegal." I cried, desperate for him not to hang up.

"Well that's where they'll be, so... sue me!"

"Please Lance, don't do me like this! I'm sorry. Talk to me please!" I begged.

"Don't do you like what? You did this to your damn self. I told you, there was nothing to talk about. You did what you did and I'm done. By the way, I'm filing for divorce, so just come get your things and you won't have to worry about me anymore."

"I told you Lance, I can't come right now. I'm in Woodville with my family," I shouted, tearfully.

"Well if you want your things bad enough you'll find a way to get back here. Bye Reina," he barked.

"Lance? Lance? Don't hang up! What about Rose, Lance?" my voice shuddered, as I called out.

The dial tone sounded and I kept calling his name, as if he were still on the line. I broke down in tears. I could not believe that he would throw my stuff outside. I tried not to topple over while standing, but my knees were very weak.

I immediately ran into the living room where Aunt Betty was and asked her for a ride back home, to retrieve my things from the house. I was embarrassed, but I did not care a thing about pride anymore, I just wanted my clothes, designer purses, jewelry, and most of all, Rose.

Aunt Betty said that she regretted not being able to bring me back home because she had choir rehearsal in the evening, but she would find someone who would and for me to just sit tight. I twiddled my thumbs impatiently at the kitchen table while she made call after call to the family members, most of which made excuses why they couldn't bring me. Finally, she hung up the phone from what she thought was good news. She had gotten me a ride.

The horn honked.

"Get on in here gal. We goin on a road trip," Uncle Sylvester said, smiling, showing off his new denture set, with his engorged belly pressing tightly up against the steering wheel.

In my mind, I already knew it was going to be the longest road trip of my life, but at least I was going home. All I could think about on the way was my Chanel purses and my Gucci boots. Many of my things I bought overseas and I cherished them just as much as the memory of being there. What was normally a beautiful ride through the country was now gloomy.

The windows were all the way down in the ninety-four Buick and the dusty wind splattered onto the side of the car, as we sailed on down the road at a speed of about thirty-five miles per hour. I tried my best not to look at Unc, as he disgustingly hawked tobacco spit into a little white cup, but kept missing the cup, instead spitting on his favorite black church slacks that he wore at least three times a week. He said that he didn't believe in drinking and driving, so he found other means to get a buzz that would not show up on a breathalyzer test.

He was having the time of his life, singing along to B.B. King on the cassette tape that played loudly. Unc knew all of the words and sang out of tune, as he held on to the wheel with both hands. I laid my head back onto the greasy headrest that he covered with plastic because Aunt Winnie had a Jeri curl.

I unbuttoned my hand me down jeans so that I could be a little more comfortable while breathing in the smell of old stale fast food that reeked throughout the car. Unc lit up a big fat Cuban cigar that he said he had been saving for a special occasion. I guess this was it.

The car started to overheat, so Unc pulled into the nearest gas station to let it cool down which was a usual occurrence according to him. He slowly got out and started looking underneath the floor mats as well as in the side of the doors to scrap up some loose change for gas.

"Unc, what are you doing?" I asked, puzzled.

"We betta get some gas while we here. I know yo pretty lil self don't wanna be pushin," he teased.

I didn't see the humor in his joke, so I just looked at him in disgust.

"Unc, are you broke?" I asked, concerned.

"Hell no, long as somebody owe you a lil change, you ain't neva broke, gal," Unc said, still laughing.

I went inside of my purse, sadly pulled out my last twenty-dollar bill and gave it to him.

"Awe, you alright gal," he happily expressed, as he took the money and headed into the store. He came out with a gallon of water, opened the hood, and started pouring. I sat there quietly in my seat, wondering if things could get any worse.

When pulling into the gated complex in which I used to live, I immediately spotted a small pile of my items. I quickly jumped out of the car and ran over to them to see what was left of my once memorable and expensive things. The black hefty duty garbage bags with the red tie strings from under our sink, ripped open and some even dumped out with my things scattered on the ground. My six hundred dollar Gucci boots were gone and so were the rest of my real expensive items, my clothes, my purses, and my jewelry. The only things left were what I was going to take to the goodwill, because they were out of season and a few other inconsequential items. I quickly beckoned Unc to help me throw the remaining bits and pieces in the back seat of the car before there would be nothing left. I went to the front door of the condo and tried to use my key, but indeed he changed the locks. I went around the back to see if by some remote chance Lance had left the door unlocked by accident, he had not.

All of a sudden, it dawned on me to check the windows because I had left them up. It was so hot in there. Lance made it there and locked them up tightly. I decided to break in, but I did not want anyone to notice me, so I went around the side to the bathroom window and to my surprise, I found it barely ajar. I guess it was an oversight on Lance's part. I looked in my purse to find a sharp object that I could use to tear through the screen. Unc helped to lift me up and push me though the very small window until I was in. I immediately ran to the front door to let Unc in. To my amazement, all of the furniture was gone along with everything else, including Rose. I stood in the middle of the desolate living room that I once occupied and bawled. I sat disorientated on the floor in dismay, as I rocked myself back and forth anxiously; waiting to wake up from what I had hoped was just a very bad dream.

Unc did not say a word. He didn't know what to say. After all, he had never been there and didn't fully understand what was going on. I had not disclosed any of the details, because I had no idea of what to expect myself.

I pulled my comatose self up and headed upstairs to the bedroom, not even stopping to wipe my tears away. Again, there were no remains of me or that we had ever lived there at all. My mind raced, my heart ached, and my body shook. I was now officially in shock.

I cried harder, which eventually amplified into an alarming scream. I struggled to catch my breath and it startled me when I began to gasp. I developed the hip ups to top it all off. My life had gone to hell in a hand basket.

"You aight up there gal," Unc hollered from the bottom of the steps, looking up?

I opened my mouth to speak, but nothing came out except distressing whimpers. Before long Unc had made his way into the bedroom to see for himself that I was okay. I sat there slumped over in a pool of my own dripping tears, with blood shot eyes and an enraged feeling of hatred towards Lance. I wanted to pick up the phone and call Uncle Seth to take care of Lance, forgetting that my cell phone was only operable for the date and time.

I looked at the clock hanging lonely on the wall, which was the only thing that Lance forgot to take. A strange feeling came over me. The clock read *three-twelve.*

I picked myself up off the floor and headed out. There was nothing left there of me, except a sheer memory. Unc kindly put his wrinkled arm around my shoulders and escorted me out. Before I buckled my seat belt, I took a deep breath and one last gaze at the condo through my passenger side window. I felt a sense of loss like never before.

On the ride back to Mississippi, I sat motionless, periodically looking back at my belongings reminding myself of what was left of my life. The ride back seemed even longer. I had cried so much earlier that there were not any tears left. My stomach felt nauseated, but nothing happened besides a little dry heaving. I had never felt so low in my entire life, not even hearing the stories of how my biological mother was a prostitute and had given me up. What am I going to do now Lord? I asked God, silently.

"Dontchu never let no man steal yo joy. I don't care what he done. You pick yoself up and keep it movin. Now I ain's no holy roller or no bible thumper, but even I know that," said Unc, trying to console me in his own way.

"It wasn't him...it was me. I did this Unc," I said, crying hysterically.

"Well, you try to fix it and if you can't then you aint got no choice but ta move on."

Unc shared his wisdom with me and drove right past Aunt Betty's house and into the parking lot of the church where Aunt Betty was hosting choir rehearsal. I did not want to go in because I knew I looked a mess. I felt a mess, but after taking a moment to think about it, I decided to go in. I thought that maybe being inside of a church again would make me feel better.

I walked in and the choir was on their feet swaying from side to side and singing hymns in unison. I immediately took a seat in the back hoping no one would notice me, but a couple of the choir members started pointing, nudging each other and waving at me. I had not seen most of them in years.

As I sat listening to the same songs from my past, I began to think, as the tears fell into my lap. My mind ran rapid with thoughts of what I could have done differently in my relationship with Lance. I should have cooked more and not complained when he had to help his family. Instead of getting mad at him when he was late, maybe I should have been more willing to let it go and enjoy the times we did spend together.

On one hand, I felt uncomfortable and out of place sitting there in my despair, but on the other hand, it was the closest thing I felt to being at home in a very long time. Aunt Betty turned around to acknowledge me with a nonjudgmental loving smile on her face while motioning to the choir to sing the chorus. I felt a sense of family again and it felt very good. I embraced it, with all I had.

After rehearsal, everyone stood in a single file line at the pulpit to grab a few finger sandwiches and some of that delicious *sweet nectar* that Aunt Betty was so famous for making. They beckoned for Unc and me to get in line to get some for ourselves and he did not waste any time running up there. I was terribly hungry by then. When I wrapped my lips around that little white Styrofoam cup, my taste buds went wild, as they used to when I was just a young girl in pigtails. That sweetened taste reminded me of family, what I had been missing for all those years that I was away.

I went into the restroom where I had not stepped foot in years, but it was still so very familiar. I never knew a toilet with a handle that you had to hold down for thirty seconds to get a proper flush could feel so close to my heart. I finished and then tore off only two squares of that rock hard toilet paper from the role, for old time's sake. I guess I wanted to pay tribute to my roots and finally embrace the place that had always embraced me.

I proudly pulled up my hand me down jeans and boldly marched my way back into the sanctuary, ate my last sandwich, gulped my last swallow and hugged everybody as if I would never see them again.

A scripture popped into my head *Train up a child in the way he should go and when he is old he shall not depart from it.*

I was right back where I started, in church, eating finger sandwiches, wearing modest clothing and a humble spirit surrounded by family and old friends whom I had forgotten that I loved so much.

THE END

# Epilogue

I sat in my pew on the left side of the church, looking at the six-foot casket, in which Mama Pearl rested. She looked angry, as if she were upset about having to die the way she did and leave her precious Lance behind. I felt rotten about the way her and I usually got along, but I took comfort in knowing that the last time I saw her was at her home and she seemed to have made peace with the fact that I was Lance's wife. I felt good that she had finally accepted me into the family. Now she was gone, and unfortunately, she never got a chance to see her grandson, Isaiah.

As I held my baby in my arms and rocked from side to side, a sudden peace came over me. I didn't feel sad, just a little mournful for Lance. Pearl was his rock and he had never been without her.

It has been one full year since I had seen him, so I decided to bring his son to the funeral to say his hellos and his goodbyes to his granny, all at the same time. He was so consumed with grief, slumped over on the front pew next to his Aunt Mae, that he barely noticed us.

After the services ended, I asked to meet him, to talk about the son he didn't know he had, and he agreed. I didn't have any expectations, really. I was happily engaged to my new fiancé, which would come as a shock as well, I'm sure.

The past year has certainly brought about some surprises. After Hurricane Katrina, I decided to get it together, finally. Life is too short for a bunch of nonsense. I'm on a mission to have that perfect life that I always dreamed of, even if it kills me....Stay Tuned...

# Acknowledgements

I am blessed to have crossed paths with all of the people that chose to support me in this project. Adrian Warren, my friend, whom I could call from dusk until dawn and was always met with your unconditional support; Frederick Sims, thank you for all of the selfless sacrifices you made for me; Steven Boyd for believing in me from the start, all of your words of encouragement really kept me motivated. A special thanks to De'ron Smith of Inspirational speaking, LLC for your mentorship and expertise. Also, I thank you Von Chaney, you were always willing to lend a helping hand at the perfect time; Thanks to David Winston of The Photo Lounge for my Author photo. Toilynn O'Neal, my cousin, thank you for the family love and support; Nicole Brewer, my best friend, you mean the world to me; Last but not least, to all of you who are fans of my work, I THANK YOU from the bottom of my heart.

Thank you God...

# About the Author

Susanna K. Green was born in Chicago, Illinois and raised in New Orleans, Louisiana. She and her immediate family evacuated New Orleans in the year 2005, due to Hurricane Katrina. She now lives in the Tampa Bay area with her son Matthew and Toy Poodle Laila.

Susanna earned a Bachelor of Arts degree in Cosmetology from the National Institute of Cosmetology and has worked in that field for over twenty years. From styling models for fashion shows to celebrity styling on movie sets; Susanna has done many great things in the industry. Susanna discovered her passion for writing, shortly after her thirtieth birthday and has since been following her new dream.

www.ingramcontent.com/pod-product-compliance
Lightning Source LLC
LaVergne TN
LVHW011224080426
835509LV00005B/304